The Proposal Writer's SWIPE FILE:

15 winning fund-raising proposals... prototypes of approaches, styles, and structures

Susan Ezell Kalish
Tara McCallum
Yvette Henry
Arnold Schoenthaler
Sheila Grady

Editors

Taft Corporation
Washington, D.C.
A member of The Taft Group

Taft Corporation, publishers of fund-raising and management information for nonprofit organizations, 5125 MacArthur Boulevard, N.W., Washington, DC 20016, (202) 966-7086.

Library of Congress Card Number 81-50258

ISBN 0-914756-45-1

OTHER ESSENTIAL TOOLS FROM TAFT...

☑ ***The 13 Most Common Fund-Raising Mistakes and How to Avoid Them***—A fund-raising classic. This down-to-earth, witty, cartoon-illustrated book shows how adherence to a few basic principles can yield more grants, more gifts, more wills and bequests. Written by Paul H. Schneiter and Donald T. Nelson, draws on exceptional experience in legendary Mormon fund-raising circles.

☑ ***The Nonprofit Executive***—Action-oriented monthly newsletter for nonprofit managers. The first newsletter dedicated to advancing the careers of executive-level nonprofit managers and development officers. Your way of keeping in touch with all trends, new development ideas, events and concepts that affect your performance and success. Features a special careers/jobs section.

☑ ***How to Rate Your Development Office: A Fund-Raising Primer for the Chief Executive***—Outstanding guide for the chief executive officer or board member who wants to gain a clearer understanding of the fund-raising process. Covers every detail needed to clarify and assess the success of a development office. Written by veteran development consultants Robert J. Berendt and J. Richard Taft.

☑ ***Dear Friend: Mastering the Art of Direct-Mail Fund Raising***—For the experienced practitioner or those just getting started in raising funds by mail. Written by Kay Partney Lautman and Henry Goldstein, senior executives of the renowned Oram Group.

☑ ***Corporate Giving Yellow Pages: Philanthropic Contact Persons for 1,100 of America's Leading Public and Privately Owned Corporations***—Lists sponsoring company, contact person, address, and phone number. Indexed by location and type of industry.

☑ ***TAFT FOUNDATION INFORMATION SYSTEM and TAFT CORPORATE INFORMATION SYSTEM***—The most sophisticated, in-depth presentations available covering all of America's major private foundations and corporate giving programs. Hardbound, 700-page directories are exhaustively indexed by area of interest, location, and by birthplace and alma mater of foundation officers and directors. Monthly newsletters update the profiles in the annual directories and supply the latest news, trends, and how-tos in the fund-raising field. Taken together, the ***Taft Corporate Information System*** and the ***Taft Foundation Information System*** comprise a complete grants-information management system called BASIC II, now used by thousands of successful nonprofit institutions.

To find out more about Taft's publications on fund raising and nonprofit management, contact:

Taft Corporation
5125 MacArthur Boulevard, N.W.
Washington, DC 20016
(202) 966-7086
(800) 424-3761

CONTENTS

INTRODUCTION

Welcome to *The Proposal Writer's Swipe File*—a handy resource book illustrating successful proposals, and giving solid examples of the fine art of proposal writing.

The proposals we have included in *Swipe File* were selected to represent the programs and approaches of a representative variety of nonprofit organizations—science, education, art, humanities, and social service. We have had to edit some material in places to keep the examples within the proper length for such a publication. Where this has occurred, we have so indicated. The proposals' tables of contents can be consulted to give the full picture, including the enclosures which we have had to omit. Specific names have been changed in all grants.

The contributors to *Swipe File* are professional proposal writers from major nonprofit organizations across the country. Their biographical sketches indicate the years of experience they represent. We are proud of their accomplishments in successful funding of important human services programs. We deeply appreciate their willingness and that of their organizations to share these proposals with our readers.

It is probably inevitable that an eventual reviewer will point out areas in which some of these proposals can be improved. We should keep in mind, however, that these are "real world" examples, actual proposals written with many different criteria (and constraints) in mind. As we review them we should remember that many different influences, many not readily apparent to the casual reviewer, are at work during the preparation of a proposal—from the funding source to the recipient organization—in such areas as style, format, time available, and individual writing styles. While it would be possible to create a hypothetical, textbook example of the "perfect" proposal, *Swipe File* readers support the value of the real thing.

Publication of this edition of *Swipe File* represents Taft's continuing focus on the need for improved professionalism in the nonprofit sector, and is another example of its commitment to providing publications and information services to help leaders in the nonprofit sector achieve that goal.

Through its newsletters, professional books, and data-based directories, Taft Corporation is doing all it can to encourage and support management improvement for nonprofits. We welcome your comments and recommendations on ways we can improve our products and services for the vast, diverse, and uniquely important nonprofit sector.

CONTRIBUTORS

Edward F. Duffy, Ph.D. Director of Development, Research and Planning, Guilford Technical Institute in Jamestown, North Carolina; former Executive Officer, Secondary Schools Aboriginal Affairs Fund, an Australian Foundation; former research associate, Office for Development, Santa Fe Community College, Gainesville, Florida; extensive experience in developing grants for secondary schools, universities, and community colleges; completed doctoral work at the University of Florida, with dissertation focusing on the characteristics and conditions of a successful community college foundation; extensive background in researching funding sources for handicapped citizens projects.

Eve Glicksman. Graduate student, Brown University; former development staff member, Corcoran Gallery of Art, Washington, D.C.; former editor, Taft Corporation; former project assistant, International Center for Social Gerontology; member, board of directors, Washington, D.C. Hotline; earned BA degree at Pennsylvania State University in broadcast journalism; plans to enter field of public radio/television with emphasis on arts and humanities programming.

Gary Johnson. Executive Director, Accounting Aid Society of Metropolitan Detroit, Michigan; former Director, National Employment and Training Assistance Program, Coopers & Lybrand, Inc., Washington, D.C.; Director Urban Resources Monitoring Projects, New Detroit, Inc., Detroit, Michigan; adjunct faculty, School of Social Work, Wayne State University; bachelor's degree in journalism, Northwestern University; MSW with emphasis on community organization and planning, University of Michigan, Ann Arbor.

Shelba Robison, Ph.D. Director, grants and resource development, Saddleback Community College, Mission Viejo, California; President, California Council for Resource Development; extensive teaching background at secondary, undergraduate, and graduate levels; bachelor of arts degree, California State University at Los Angeles; masters and doctoral degrees in government and urban studies, Claremont Graduate School.

A. Lin Stefurak, Ph.D. Assistant Vice President, Triton College, River Grove, Illinois; extensive experience in grantsmanship and resource development; ten years of administrative experience from public school to college level; consultant to public school districts, colleges, and universities in areas of resource development for community programming; 52 successfully funded projects for over $3 million during last three years; Vice-President & President-elect, National Council for Resource Development; master's degree in education from the University of South Florida at Tampa; doctoral degree from the University of Florida, Gainesville.

Jeffrey A. Stuckman, Ed.D. Director, Institutional Research, Florida Junior College at Jacksonville for over 12 years; member, board of directors, Florida Council for Resource Development; charter member, National Council for Resource Development (NCRD); member, NCRD Categorical Aid Task Force; earned doctoral degree at University of Florida; earned bachelor and master's degrees at Ohio State University.

Stephen R. Wise, Ed.D. Executive Director, Educational Resource Development, Florida Junior College at Jacksonville; former Executive Director, Florida Junior College Foundation; Chairman, board of directors, Opportunities Development, Inc; charter member, board of directors, National Association of Public Service Organization Executives (NAPSOE); member and past Director, National Council for Resource Development; board member, Jacksonville Council on Citizen Involvement; past President, Florida Council for Resource Development.

Social Welfare
Civic

HANDICAPPED ADVOCACY PROJECT
to run from
April 1, 1980 to September 30, 1980
submitted by
Austin Technical Institute

Project Director:
Bill Blama
Director of Development, Research and Planning
Austin Technical Institute
P.O. Box 301 Jamesburg, North Carolina 27846

PURPOSE

Elizabeth County has a sizable handicapped population (more than 1,000 persons). The Elizabeth County Consortium serves a small percentage of this population (less than 2 percent). It is the purpose of this proposal to establish a CETA Handicapped Advocacy project that will enable a large number of the handicapped to be served by the consortium.

The personnel for this project will gather data regarding the handicapped population in Elizabeth County as well as the CETA services being provided to this group. The project personnel will develop a service delivery model to better serve the needs of the handicapped in Elizabeth County. Finally, the personnel will develop a resource manual for community college and CETA administrators, outlining resources and a service delivery model.

OBJECTIVES

A. Identify the Elizabeth County handicapped population and its characteristics.

B. Identify agencies serving the handicapped in Elizabeth County.

C. Identify and analyze the characteristics of CETA-certified handicapped persons in Elizabeth County.

D. Identify those barriers to handicapped persons' participation in CETA programs.

E. Establish a resource library for Austin Institute faculty to assist CETA handicapped students.

F. Establish an advocacy office for the handicapped at Austin Institute.

G. Review assessment processes established for the handicapped and establish model evaluative procedures for at least five handicapped categories.

H. Facilitate the access of CETA handicapped students to all CETA programs.

I. Develop a transportation system for handicapped students at Austin Institute.

J. Develop a model service delivery system for CETA-eligible handicapped students.

K. Distribute the developed model and resource manual to personnel concerned with CETA programs in Elizabeth County and in the North Carolina Community

L.   Gather data regarding the needs of the handicapped by counseling handicapped CETA students or prospective students.

M.   Investigate and analyze effective methods of recruiting handicapped students to CETA programs.

N.   Orient CETA personnel, Austin Institute faculty, and counselors to the needs of the handicapped.

O.   Develop procedures to facilitate the entry of CETA handicapped students to a broad range of training programs.

P.   Establish an advisory committee made up of representatives of social agency personnel, CETA staff, and Austin Institute faculty and staff to facilitate the success of the project.

PROJECT DESCRIPTION

The project will run six months. The project will be run by a coordinator and one secretary. The tasks of the project will be divided accordingly:

1.   Gather basic data

    a.   Handicapped population

    b.   CETA services

    c.   Other handicapped services

2.   Visiting exemplary models for the handicapped

3.   Consult with handicapped students and develop an effective recruitment system

4.   Develop resource manual and model delivery system

5.   Refine resource and delivery system

6.   Produce final developed resource manual

7.   Disseminate developed document and establish procedures to better serve the handicapped at Austin Institute

8.   Evaluate project

The following will be involved in the project:

Austin Institute and staff, especially counselors; CETA occupational specialist; and the CETA special services staff

The staff of the Elizabeth County Consortium and contracting CETA agencies

The CETA program staffs of community colleges in North Carolina

Representatives from agencies serving the handicapped in Elizabeth County

LINKAGE

The project coordinator will involve the advisory council representatives from Elizabeth County public and private agencies. Representatives from CETA contracting agencies will also be consulted. The coordinator will examine strategies used by school systems and the community college system that will eliminate barriers for the handicapped to CETA programs. Experts within the community will be consulted to determine the applicability of strategies found at other institutions.

EVALUATION

A consultant will be used at the beginning and at the end of the project to facilitate its evaluation. This person will be used at the beginning of the project to refine the objectives of the project and to give direction to the advisory council and to the project coordinator.

The advisory council will meet at least three times during the period of the grant to evaluate the progress made and to assist the coordinator.

The consultant in the final report will evaluate the project based on the successful completion at the refined project objectives as well as the completed model and resource manual.

BUDGET OUTLINE

I.	Staff Costs and Fringe Benefits	$15,476.94
II.	Staff Travel	1,500.00
III.	Training Costs	0.00
IV.	Equipment Costs	2,000.00
V.	Office Supplies and Materials	500.00
VI.	Communications	800.00
VII.	Other	
	a. Consultants	1,200.00
	b. Publications	2,000.00
	c. Instructional Supplies	800.00
	Subtotal	$24,276.94
VIII.	Indirect Costs	1,942.16
	Grand Total	$26,219.10

DISPLACED HOMEMAKER DEVELOPMENT GRANT

Development Grant - Displaced Homemaker
to run from
April 1, 1980 to July 31, 1980
submitted by
Ellard Technical Institute

DEFINITION OF PROBLEM

Over 65 percent of the people served by the Three-County Consortium are women. A large percentage of these women are displaced homemakers. CETA legislation as well as recent research have highlighted the special needs of this population. Women reaching midlife, roughly late thirties to fifties, encounter a number of major life crises that are physiological, psychological, and sociological in nature, which makes adjusting or even coping very difficult.

There is a need to take a hard look at what happens to women in their middle years and on. They are experiencing low self-esteem, role conflicts, guilt, depression, fear, and loneliness. A homemaker's self-confidence must be raised to overcome fear of entering the job market. Since the homemaker is generally a novice in the labor market, she needs an orientation to the world of work and help to obtain a job. These and other facts prove the need for cooperative action to integrate women fully into the economic structure, because the alternative is apt to include a high incidence of nonproductivity and wasted talent and to keep the tax base smaller than it could be. In turn, those conditions will affect local markets and sales, the ability of government to finance public services, and the city's effort to develop additional economic opportunities.

Although many services are available to displaced homemakers in Ellard County, there is a need to coordinate these services to meet the special needs of the CETA-eligible displaced homemakers.

DESCRIPTION OF PROJECT

The project will develop a plan to establish a women's resource center. The resource center will establish a tailored program to assist displaced homemakers with the transition into the workforce. The primary target population is the community's economically disadvantaged females. The project will provide services so the participants can receive appropriate training and obtain jobs to become self-sufficient. It will assist business, industry, education, service agencies, and government in identifying employment and its training needs and will create linkages with supportive services.

GOALS AND OBJECTIVES

Goals

This project will:

1. Collect data on the needs of displaced homemakers in Ellard County and the placements of displaced homemakers centers.

2. Analyze the data and the service delivery system in Ellard County for the displaced homemaker.
3. Develop a model service delivery system for the displaced homemaker in the county.

Objectives

The coordinator, in developing the project for Ellard County, will:

1. Establish a list of resources for the displaced homemaker in the county.
2. Develop a profile of the displaced homemaker in Ellard County.
3. Develop a prioritized list of the needs of the displaced homemaker in the county.
4. Review the present centers established in the county to meet the needs of women.
5. Develop a system to serve the needs of displaced homemakers.
6. Survey business, industry, education, employment resources, service agencies, and existing programs to establish an effective job readiness and job placement program for this population.
7. Work with the staff of CETA contracting agencies to establish a coordinated plan to meet the needs of the displaced homemaker.
8. Develop a system to place women in nontraditional job alternatives.
9. Develop an evaluation program for the proposed resource center.
10. Develop an advisory council made up of representatives of social service agencies, educational institutions, and industry.
11. Work cooperatively with the displaced homemakers center in High View.

ADMINISTRATOR

Description

Overall, the administrator will direct the program, overseeing both day-to-day management and long-range planning. Specific job responsibilities include the following:

1. Establishing the needs of displaced homemakers
2. Reviewing CETA programs in light of the needs of the displaced homemaker
3. Devising long-range plans for meeting the needs of the displaced homemaker
4. Establishing links with other Ellard Technical Institute program personnel and devising and implementing guidelines to utilize and integrate existing services
5. Establishing ties with those community services, businesses, and industries in developing the program
6. Establishing links with other displaced homemakers programs in the county and state.

5. Establishing ties with those community services, businesses, and industries in developing the program

6. Establishing links with other displaced homemakers programs in the county and state.

Qualifications

This person should have a working knowledge of career counseling and/or job training programs and some knowledge of the target population.

This position will require a person with proven skills in the areas of program planning and management, personnel administration, and public relations. The administrator should be able to establish relationships with community services, business, industry, and educational resources and effectively enlist their cooperation to meet program objectives.

A bachelor's degree in administration, social sciences, or a related field and experience in the skills-related areas are required.

SECRETARY

Description

This person will perform various secretarial duties for the administrator and other program personnel. He/she will handle the clerical and general office work. The secretary also will establish and maintain a filing system for the program. Additional secretarial functions may be assigned by the administrator.

Qualifications

Applicant must have proficient general office and secretarial skills, including an excellent typing ability (approximately 60 wpm). This individual must be personable and be able to effectively work with others, including program participants. Applicant must be a good organizer, be highly initiative, and be able to work without close supervision.

High school diploma or GED certificate required; postsecondary training and experience are desirable.

BUDGET OUTLINE

I. Staff Costs and Fringe Benefits

	Salary	FICA	Retirement	Hospitalization	Annual Leave
Coordinator	$4,833.33	$296.28	$440.80	$105.28	$159.02
Secretary	3,000.00	183.90	273.60	105.28	98.70
	$7,833.33	$480.18	$714.40	$210.56	$257.72

Total Staff Costs and Fringe Benefits	$9,496.19
II. Staff Travel	1,600.00
III. Equipment Costs	2,300.00
IV. Office Supplies and Materials	500.00
V. Communications	900.00
VI. Other	

Consultant	$ 800.00	
Publications	1,000.00	1,800.00

Project Total	$16,596.19

VII.   Indirect Cost (8%)   1,327.70

GRAND TOTAL $17,923.89

Implementation: Interinstitutional Model for the Delivery of

Programs and Services for the Aging

Submitted to:

Oregon Board of Regents

by

Office for Community Education

College of Education

University of Oregon

TABLE OF CONTENTS

PROJECT ABSTRACT

An increasing population of older citizens in Oregon demands a new and comprehensive format for the delivery of continuing education programs and basic human services. National and state policy statements stress the need for educational institutions, public service agencies, and volunteer organizations to effectively coordinate their resources to find new and creative ways of cooperative delivery of community services and continuing education to the aging population. An identifiable need exists to jointly target educational and community service resources toward a cooperative systematic approach to:

1. Identifying needs

2. Setting and prioritizing goals

3. Developing a plan of action for delivery

4. Implementing programs and services

5. Evaluating, resulting in the delivery of effective and targeted community services for the aging.

The purpose of this project is to implement the interinstitutional "process model" for the delivery of programs and services for the aging, presently being developed under the current Higher Education Act (HEA) Title I Project, in three selected Oregon communities. In addition, the existing coordinating council will implement the plan of action for increased programs and services.

To accomplish this purpose three communities in the state will be se-

19

lected for implementation of the model. The three sites will be urban, suburban with a high-density elderly population, and rural. Upon identification of sites the agency administrators will be identified and contacted concerning the proposed project. Participating agencies and institutions will form coordinating councils. Upon formation of the councils a survey will be conducted to assess the existing level of coordination and cooperative delivery of services. Once the councils have been formed and surveyed, the interagency process model will be implemented. A cooperative system for need assessment will be undertaken. From this assessment goals will be identified and prioritized. Based upon this process a plan of action will be developed for meeting the goals. Each agency or institution will address those goals for which it is best suited. The cooperative programs and services will be implemented in the three communities. Concurrently, the project staff will provide the necessary training to facilitate the adoption of the model process. In addition, the data will be collected and processed to provide information for evaluation of the implementation process.

Through the implementation and validation of this process model a new step will be taken to enhance the efforts of institutions and agencies serving the needs of the aging population in Oregon.

NEED

A new group consciousness is developing across the country among the more than forty million persons 55 years of age and over. Whether they go by the name of senior citizens, the aging, the elderly, or older Americans, they share common priorities of seeking new definitions to life-long development and involvement. Older people constitute the fastest growing segment of Oregon's population. According to recent census figures, Oregon's elderly population is growing twice as rapidly as its total population. As a group, however, they have not benefited from the educational and personal services available to their younger counterparts. Steps have been taken to move schools and colleges away from traditional classroom settings, school yards, and campuses and into the community arena. However, secondary school systems, community colleges, senior institutions, and community-based service organizations must shape new networks of cooperation and coordinated action to jointly target their educational and service resources toward the specific community service needs of the growing population of older people.

National and state policy statements stress the need for educational institutions, public service agencies, and volunteer organizations to effectively coordinate their resources to find new and creative ways of cooperative delivery of community services and continuing education to the aging population. An identifiable need exists to jointly target educational and community service resources toward a cooperative systematic approach to: 1) identifying needs; 2) setting and prioritizing goals; 3) developing a plan of action for delivery; 4) implementing programs and services; and 5) evaluating, resulting in the delivery of effective and targeted community services for the aging.

The older Americans have been isolated socially, denied opportunities for educational growth or cultural and recreational enrichment. There is a tremendous opportunity to focus major attention upon the special problems of the aging and to enhance the delivery of educational and personal services to the aging through a coordinated multiagency approach.

The University of Oregon Center for Community Education is presently conducting an HEA Title I Project which is developing an administrative design for coordinated cooperative delivery of services for the aging. The interinstitutional coordinating council for this project consists of the: 1) dean of community and evening programs at Lorren Community College; 2) director, program development, division of continuing education; 3) administrator, Squarrell County Division of Social Services; 4) Aging and Adult Services Supervisor for HRS; 5) director for community education, Squarrell County Schools; 6) executive director, Squarrell County Older Americans Council; 7) adult services supervisor, social and economic services, HRS; 8) administrator, Social Security Administration; and 9) state director, National Retired Teachers Association. They have identified the implicit need for their professional colleagues in other communities in Oregon to be trained and involved in the process model for developing interinstitutional/agency programs and services for the aging (see Appendix B).

The council has recognized the necessity to field test the developing model in communities that are urban; suburban, with a high-density elderly population; and rural, to establish replicability and validity for utilization of the model on a statewide basis   (see Appendix B).

PURPOSE

The primary purpose of this project is to implement the interinstitutional process model for the delivery of programs and services for the aging, presently being developed under current HEA Title I Project, in three selected communities in Oregon. In each of the three communities it will specifically address itself to:

- Maximizing the collective facilities, personnel, financial resources, and coordinated educational programs of the educational institutions and service agencies for the aging in the community.

- Encouraging and promoting planned systematic and continuous participation of senior citizens in the delivery of educational and service opportunities.

- Providing training and professional development for institutional staff and personnel, community service staffs, and selected lay citizens from aging services.

- Developing public policy-making frameworks conducive to the planning and promotion of effective programs delivering services for the aging in their particular settings.

- Validating the functional process model, capable of being further replicated on a statewide basis, for coordinated training and delivery of programs and services for the aging.

In addition, the existing interinstitutional/agency coordinating council, established under the current HEA Title I grant, will expand program offerings for the aging population based upon the plan of action developed the first year.

GOALS AND OBJECTIVES

I.   Implementation of the Interinstituional Model for the Delivery of
Programs and Services for the Aging in three target areas--

  A.   To identify the appropriate institutional and agency administra-
       tors in the three selected communities.

  B.   To assess the current level of coordination and cooperation for
       the delivery of services in the selected communities.

  C.   To form interinstitutional/agency coordinating councils in each
       of the selected communities.

  D.   To implement the interinstitutional/agency process model for the
       delivery of programs and services for the aging in the selected
       communities.

  E.   To continue the development of the existing Squarrell County
       Interistitutional Coordinating Council established under current
       HEA Title I grant.

  F.   To collect data for evaluation of the implementation process.

II. Expansion of program offerings by the Squarrell County Interinstitutional
Agency Coordinating Council.

  A.   Implementation of the plan of action for increased programs and
       services developed under the current HEA Title I Project.

  B.   Expansion of cooperatively offered programs and services for the
       aging population of Squarrell County.

PROCEDURES

This project will commence on July 1, 1980 and terminate on June 30, 1981. It will be conducted in two phases, as described below.

The project will draw on the resources of the University of Oregon and the cooperating institutions and agencies in the three implemantation sites as well as those in Squarrell County.

The three implementation sites were selected upon their qualifying under the criteria established to field test the model. Individuals in leadership positions within the identified communities have been involved in the development of this project plan. These individuals have volunteered to serve as ad hoc committee chairpersons to establish interinstitutional/agency coordinating councils in their communities. Additionally, to maximize the implementation results, the chairpersons of each of the ad hoc committees are associated with different administrative positions and/or institutions (see Appendix E).

In addition, a 1980-81 chairperson will be elected by the existing Squarrell County Interinstitutional/Agency Coordinating Council in June of 1980 to assure leadership in implementing the established plan of action as developed under the current HEA Title I Project.

During the first month the chairpersons and their respective ad hoc committees will be provided with preservice training regarding the goals and objectives of the project. Steps will be initiated to develop a specific methodology for recording data to be used for summative and formative evaluation procedures as the project progresses. A project journal will be established to contain information providing data for intermediate evaluation, and a project monograph will be published the twelfth month.

During the second month each of the ad hoc committees will develop a comprehensive interinstitutional/agency coordinating council for the delivery of programs and services for the aging. These councils will consist of appropriate institution and agency administrators who will have primary responsibility for their institution's or agency's participation in the project. The administrative design of the model will be adapted to complement local situations. Provisions will be made to ensure that the councils will continue to operate upon the termination of the funded project.

Also during the second month an evaluation format for this project will be designed. The methodology will consist of techniques for formative and summative evaluation. Questionnaires will be developed to gather information from the participants on the programs and services provided in the three communities. These questionnaires will be used in conjunction with interviews and observations to provide ongoing evaluation. A project evaluation team comprised of council members and program staff members will be selected to conduct mid-point and final evaluations to provide information for each activity unit and for the summative evaluation of the project.

IMPLEMENTATION

The three interinstitutional/agency coordinating councils for the delivery of programs and services for the aging in the selected communities will compile and analyze existing needs assessment information to determine the needs of the aging in their respective areas. Also, a needs assessment instrument will be constructed and administered. Concurrently, the existing council will determine the human, physical, and financial resources of the participating institutions and agencies available to meet the needs of the aging.

The project staff with assistance from the currently established HEA Title I Squarrell County Interinstitutional/Agency Coordinating Council will provide techincal assistance in assessing and determining the existing cooperation and coordination of programs and services for the aging among the participating councils, as well as in identifying areas of limited coordination and cooperation that may result in the duplication or lack of programs and services. Further, technical assistance will be provided for the training and professional development of the council members and their respecitve staffs. This training will emphasize development of skills needed to promote coordination and cooperation among the participating institutions and agencies. The training sessions may vary in duration from one to five days and will include, but not be limited to, the following activities and/ or skills:

1. Needs assessment skills
2. Problem-solving skills
3. Goal-setting skills
4. Planning skills
5. Interpersonal skills
6. System diagnosis skills

7. Evaluation procedures

8. Program and goal achievement methodologies

9. Techniques in leadership and resource development

Based upon the needs assessment data and the survey of the project staff, all four of the project councils will develop a plan of action to initiate and expand coordinated and cooperative programs and services for the aging. Each council will establish ad hoc committees to draft formal public policies to support their cooperative endeavors. Additionally, they will develop strategies for the implementation of these policies for increased delivery of interinstitutional/agency programs and services for the aging. The three new coordinating councils will then utilize these strategies to implement the adoption of policies within their respective institutions or agencies.

Upon completion of this activity specific program roles and responsibilities will be identified. Accountability and evaluation procedures for programs and services will be established, and specific programs will be implemented according to the established plan of action to develop aging services in areas such as income, housing, nutrition, consumer education, health care, transportation, and leisure activities. An initial publication listing these cooperative programs and services in each community will be published and provided to aging population.

Concurrent with the procedures for the three expansion sites, the Squarrell County Interinstitutional/Agency Coordinating Council will be involved with implementation if the plan of action developed under the current HEA Title I grant. This plan will allow for the expansion of program offerings by the individual institutions and agencies and for the institution of additional programs and services provided through cooperative arrangements. Also, the project staff will provide training to additional staff members of the participating organizations who have not been previously involved under the initial training program.

During the latter part of the project a monograph will be developed and published describing the project design and implementation. The monograph will be distributed on a statewide basis and selectively on a national basis by the University of Oregon Center for Community Education.

EVALUATION

The evaluation of the components of the project will be designed based on the purposes of the project. These purposes will be articulated during the initial planning process. A comprehensive evaluation will involve at least the following components:

1. The project staff will establish performance objectives for participants involved in the project. This will provide evaluation oversight and direction for each segment of the project.

2. In each of the four communities teams of community research personnel will be selected to review the project and its impact on the local aging population on a quarterly basis. These teams will be selected for their expertise in specific areas such as

business, social services, educational services and the aging.

Additionally, in the last month of the project a state Title I director (T.B.A.) from another state will be selected as a consultant to provide
on-site visitation to each of the four participating communities and to
confer with the four councils and project staff. The outside consultant
will prepare a summative evaluation report of the project. Further, outside
evaluation will involve members of the Oregon HEA Title I Staff and Oregon
Title I Advisory Council.

BUDGET JUSTIFICATION

The project will have an administrative director (on a part-time basis
at no cost to the project) who will oversee the project activities and provide liaison services among the several colleges of the University of Oregon.
Project activities will be managed by a full-time project coordinator home-
based at the university (see Appendix G). Additional project assistance
will be provided by a one-fourth time graduate assistant (T.B.A.) to help
with program development, services, and training, in conjunction with the
assistance (at no cost to the project) of the graduate assistant from the
Center for Community Education. A secretarial position will be provided also
at no cost to the project.

Travel

Primary travel expenditures will be in the planning and delivery of
services and educational programs to the three participating communities.

Printing

A project monograph will be developed and disseminated to all 67 public school districts, 28 community colleges, the twelve state universities, and the various private colleges and universities in the state. In addition, the monograph will be distributed to all health and rehabilitative services divisions of aging district offices, the state's Older Americans Councils, district area agencies on aging, regional offices of social service agencies, and other selected institutions and agencies.

Other

The four chairpersons from the ad hoc committees and the Squarrell County Interinstitutional/Agency Council will be awarded a $500.00 direct subcontract to cover administrative costs incurred in the implementation of this project.

ESTIMATED BUDGET FISCAL YEAR 1980

STAFF AND FACULTY Position or Title	Monthly Salary	% Time	COST Institution	Federal	Total
Project Director	$ 2,109.00	25	$6,327.00	$ -0-	$ 6,327.00
Project Coordinator	1,673.00	100	3,000.00	17,071.00	20,071.00
Graduate Assistant (1/3)	347.00	25	1,040.00	-0-	1,040.00
Graduate Assistant (1/4)	260.00	100	-0-	3,120.00	3,120.00
Secretary	612.00	33.3	2,424.00	-0-	2,424.00
EMPLOYEE BENEFITS (15.5%)					
Graduate Assistant Employee Benefits .0065%			1,828.00	2,667.00	4,495.00
Health Insurance: $18.00 per month					
Project Director			54.00	-0-	54.00
Project Coordinator			-0-	216.00	216.00
Project Secretary			72.00	-0-	72.00
CONSULTANT			150.00	50.00	200.00
TRAVEL					
Project Director			250.00	-0-	250.00
Project Coordinator			200.00	900.00	1,100.00
Graduate Assistants (2)			100.00	300.00	400.00
Ad Hoc Committee Chairpersons (4)			100.00	400.00	500.00
Consultant			150.00	50.00	200.00
PRINTING AND SUPPLIES			150.00	300.00	450.00
TELEPHONE			120.00	580.00	700.00
INSTRUCTIONAL AND MEDIA MATERIALS			-0-	100.00	100.00
OTHER COST					
Subcontract grants to the four ad hoc committees			-0-	2,000.00	2,000.00
State Department of Administration Personnel Assessment @ $8.00/FTE/Quarter on Career Service Personnel (Secretary)			11.00	-0-	11.00
SUBTOTAL COST				27,754.00	43,730.00
OVERHEAD 8%				2,220.00	2,220.00
TOTAL COST			$15,976.00	$29,974.00	$45,950.00

B U D G E T

	Percentage of Time	Number of Months	Title VIII	Non-Title VIII	Total
SALARIES					
Project Director	10%	12	$ -0-	$ 2,000	$ 2,000
Co-op Director	100%	12	$20,000	$ -0-	$20,000
Faculty Co-op Coordinators (5)	25%	12	$15,000	$ 6,000	$21,000
Co-op Coordinator/Job Developer	100%	12	$15,000	$ -0-	$15,000
Project Secretary	100%	12	$ 9,150	$ -0-	$ 9,150
Counselors	10%	12	$ -0-	$ 2,000	$ 2,000
Consultants (10 days @ $100/day)			$ 1,000	$ -0-	$ 1,000
SUBTOTAL			$60,150	$10,000	$70,150
FRINGE BENEFITS 22% (estimate) SUBTOTAL			$ 1,301*	$ 220	$ 1,521
TRAVEL					
Local (employer visitation/student supervision)			$ 1,000	$ -0-	$ 1,000
Professional Conferences/Training			$ 500	$ -0-	$ 500
Consultant Travel (estimate)			$ 1,000	$ -0-	$ 1,000
CEA National Meeting			$ 500	$ -0-	$ 500
SUBTOTAL			$ 3,000	$ -0-	$ 3,000
OTHER					
Photocopying			$ -0-	$ 200	$ 200
Printing			$ 1,000	$ -0-	$ 1,000
Office Supplies			$ 250	$ 250	$ 500
Postage			$ 300	$ 200	$ 500
Telephone			$ 350	$ -0-	$ 350
SUBTOTAL			$ 1,900	$ 650	$ 2,550
TOTAL			$66,351	$10,870	$77,221
INDIRECT COSTS - 8%			$ 5,280	$ -0-	$ 5,280
TOTAL PROJECT COSTS			$71,631	$10,870	$82,501

*Based on $59,150 less $1,000 consultants' fee.

33

ORGANIZATIONAL SUPPORT: ACCOUNTING AID SOCIETY

A PROPOSAL TO FUND

PROFESSIONAL ACCOUNTING ASSISTANCE

FOR NONPROFIT ORGANIZATIONS

PRESENTED BY

THE ACCOUNTING AID SOCIETY OF METROPOLITAN DETROIT

TABLE OF CONTENTS

I. GOALS AND OBJECTIVES

Our primary goal in establishing the Accounting Aid Society of Metropolitan Detroit is to aid nonprofit groups in the establishment of a comprehensive system of accounting procedures in order to satisfy their accounting and bookkeeping responsibilities to the Internal Revenue Service, funding organizations, and the public. The objectives we plan to pursue to accomplish this goal will be to assess the present accounting system; to prepare and implement, if necessary, new accounting and management systems; and to train the staff of the nonprofit group in the use of these systems. We also plan to monitor the group to determine if staff skills have improved and if the new systems have been properly and efficiently applied. All services will be offered free of charge to any client who can demonstrate need and an inability to pay.

Further, we will be available to assist citizens of this area with such services as instruction in bank reconciliations, budgeting of resources, debt consolidation, and the use of checks and tax services. To accomplish this we plan to involve the faculties of the local universities as well as specialists from public agencies and private industry.

AAS-MD will also give Detroit area accountants and financial executives the opportunity to use their skills to social advantage. This will serve to acquaint Detroit residents with the professionalism of our members as well.

Finally, our goal is to aid local accounting students by giving them an opportunity to receive real-life experience by using the tools they are acquiring in the classroom. It is hoped that the closer examination of the accounting profession offered by AAS will serve to increase the quantity and quality of the students who seek a career in accounting.

We plan to use the services of volunteers in a most efficient way. A counseling team of one professional volunteer and one or more student volunteers will be assigned to each case. These volunteers will be aided by a preassignment process that includes orientation, preservice training in model systems, case study analysis, and self-evaluation studies. A programmed manual has been developed to assure consistently high quality service.

II. EVALUATION OF GOALS AND OBJECTIVES

Inasmuch as we cannot measure the success of our assistance in terms of profit or loss (surplus or deficit), we must measure that success in terms of:

1. The adequacy of our documentation of the system (flow charts, block diagrams and/or procedures) which we design and install for the client

2. The adequacy of the training we give the client
   as measured by the ability of that client to
   successfully maintain the improved system
   without further aid.

System support will entail the design and installation, as required, of
(1) system of cash receipts, (2) system of cash disbursements, (3) property
accounting systems, (4) payroll systems, (5) chart of accounts, and
(6) petty cash system.

Client training will consist of the preparation of simplified written
procedures and instructions to client personnel on the implementation of
these procedures. Follow-up will be conducted at specified periods
subsequent to the completion of the initial training session.

Finally, in order to insure that all facets of the organization's
operation have been examined, recommendations will be made detailing any
problems observed during the course of our intervention. These recommendations will cover overall administrative and financial management of
the client organization.

III. IMPLEMENTATION

A. Specific Needs

We are aware that there are many nonprofit groups and private individuals in the metropolitan Detroit area who need accounting/bookkeeping
assistance. Without an organization like the Accounting Aid Society of
Metropolitan Detroit (AAS-MD) most of these organizations would be unable to
secure and efficiently utilize financial assistance. The existing system of
providing accounting aid is incapable of satisfying the ever-increasing demand.

In fact, various funding agencies whose service delivery systems include
community-based organizations frequently find that these groups have in-
adequate accounting/bookkeeping systems. This results in an inability to
satisfy the administrative requirements of their subcontract. These in-
adequate systems also undermine the efficiency and effectiveness of the
group and cause organizations to spend an inordinate amount of time keeping
up with the paperwork to satisfy the grant requirements.

Also, with an ineffective or informal accounting system the organization
does not know if it is using its resources efficiently. Cost-effectiveness
figures cannot be generated without accurate data and the systems necessary
to evaluate them. Finally, the lack of an accounting system proves to be
detrimental to the morale of the organization's staff. Inadequacy of such a
central function as the bookkeeping system means delay in processing payments
and in reimbursing employees.

B. Client Market

As a result of the recognition of these needs AAS-MD has contacted potential referral agencies--agencies that are subcontracting with, or have program relationships with, organizations that have these problems. Organizations like the Professional Skills Alliance (PSA) and New Detroit, Inc. (NDI), have told AAS-MD that there are approximately 300 organizations requiring the support and assistance of AAS-MD. (Please refer to Section D of the Appendix.) Once other groups and organizations know what is available, the demand for our services will increase significantly, particularly if public service announcements are used.

C. The Client - AAS Process

1. Orientation Preservice Training. Before volunteer professionals and students are assigned to the client a preliminary orientation will be provided. Preservice training will require a full day's instruction in the use of our programmed systems. This system is composed of two parts--the learning guide and the client assistance guide.

The programmed learning guide will include descriptions of various skills and techniques to allow the volunteers to quickly evaluate the new client and place the organization in the proper category of need. The programmed guide will continue to demonstrate our understanding of client needs as reflected by our past experiences with groups in need of accounting/ bookkeeping assistance.

A programmed manual or client assistance guide has been designed to accomplish the following tasks:

-Provide a baseline evaluation of the present system

-Provide a baseline evaluation of the bookkeeping skills of client personnel

-Estimate dollar value of services

-Suggest a course of skills upgrading

-Outline follow-up procedures

Professional accountants representing AAS-MD, PSA, and the Michigan Association of Certified Public Accountants have been involved in the establishment of our programmed system. These same people will make a special effort to reevaluate this system and the procedures it establishes so as to incorporate the latest techniques found to be useful with new clients.

Also included in our preservice training of volunteers is a study of the model systems and procedures already found to be effective in past cases.

Several case studies have been selected for review by our volunteers to acquaint them with the scope of our program. (See Appendix B for summaries.)

Finally, the volunteers undergo a private self-evaluation that will incorporate a value analysis and a written report to examine the area of personal social responsibility. This is important, we feel, in order to crystalize in the mind of the volunteer the reasons for which he or she has chosen to provide his or her skills without economic reward. At the completion of this preservice training the volunteer will be assigned to a specific case that reflects his or her areas of specialization and interest.

2. Referral. A preliminary assessment form will be prepared by the referral agency (or by us under certain circumstances) and shall serve to establish the extent of the client's need and the client's inability to pay for such services from the for-profit sector.

At this point the AAS will provide the client with consultation and technical assistance. While there are some requests that we will be unable to satisfy, we will be capable of offering assistance in the areas of:

-Establishing bookkeeping systems

-Training in bookkeeping techniques

-Preparing taxes for indigent families

-Training in personal budgeting

-Referring clients to other volunteer assistance programs

3. Intervention. Once a client is accepted as eligible (has proved need and inability to pay) and is assigned a volunteer team of one professional accountant and at least one student, the intervention process begins. An assessment of present capability is made to serve as a baseline from which a fiscal accounting and management plan can be developed. This baseline or present position can be accurately determined by the use of the evaluation process spelled out in the programmed manual. In most cases, however, the present accounting system will be insufficient or nonexistent.

The volunteer team will initiate a predesigned process for improvement, outlined in the client assistance manual, to upgrade both the present bookkeeping system and the skills of at least two members of the client organization. Model systems and procedures have already been designed that maximize skills in a minimum amount of time. Proper use and understanding of ledgers, journals, source documents, statements, and generally accepted accounting principles will be taught in order to insure eventual self-sufficiency.

Other prepackaged systems can be presented and employed as resources permit. Seminars on tax preparation, bank reconciliations, and budget preparation could be offered to the public by professional volunteers from university faculties and from the professional accounting and business communities.

4. Monitoring. In order to keep all interested parties appraised of a client's progress, an ongoing monitoring program will be employed. This will include periodic evaluations (at 3, 6, and 12 months, or as needed) by the accounting team and the executive director. Monitoring of this type indicates whether or not the fiscal accounting and management objectives established by the team are being reached. Progress reports will be supplied to AAS, the referring agency, and the funding source.

Contact with the funding source (and/or referral agency) is particularly important, since the practical results of the AAS intervention must satisfy its requirements.

5. Evaluation. At the end of the intervention period a final evaluation will be done to determine the degree of improvement in the organization's accounting and management procedures. This will be accomplished with the use of the programmed manual. Particular attention will be paid to insuring that the client has mastered a sufficient amount of technical accounting in order to assure a self-maintaining system.

The impact of our assistance will be analyzed by comparing the final evaluation with the baseline study. A detailed determination of the total number of hours donated by both the professional and student volunteers will be done. This will allow AAS to do an efficiency evaluation of our service and will aid in future estimation of required volunteer needs relative to specific client needs.

6. Debriefing. Finally, a debriefing process will be accomplished at a meeting of the volunteers and the executive director. This meeting will be designed to highlight the techniques employed and the level of success. Over time it is felt that this will aid us in determining the best approach in various situations. At this time AAS will report back to the funding source and/or referring agency and terminate the active phase of our involvement with the client. Although we will be available for further consultation, proper training during the intervention process will hold this to a minimum.

D. Associated Activities

1. Grantor briefings will be available to potential grantees in order to better acquaint them with the requirements of prospective grantors.

2. Seminars, both lecture and discussion types, will be offered as resources permit. Many facets of bookkeeping, accounting, management, administrative, and marketing techniques will serve as subjects. Past, present, and prospective clients will be invited as their needs suggest.

3. Financial forecasting and feasibility services will be offered in order to satisfy management needs and grantor requirements.

4. Internal control reviews and recommendations will be offered to those groups who already practice acceptable accounting systems but desire periodic reevaluation to determine the adequacy of their systems.

IV. ADMINISTRATION-MANAGEMENT PLAN

The Accounting Aid Society of Metropolitan Detroit (AAS-MD) is presently seeking tax-exempt status from the Internal Revenue Service. In the meantime New Detroit, Inc., will serve as our fiduciary.

AAS-MD will be supervised by a board of directors comprised of 24 people from many segments of the community. Special care has been taken to include persons from both public and private accounting organizations, professional accounting associations, the local universities, and other community organizations. (Please refer to Section F of the Appendix.)

The board will meet quarterly to develop policy positions and recommend procedures for operation. A six-member executive committee will meet as needed (approximately monthly) to assist the executive director.

The executive director will be a qualified individual having experience not only in accounting matters but also in administrative and social problems. (Please refer to Section C of the Appendix for a more complete job description for the executive director.)

The university coordinators will be accounting professors or representatives from local universities, appointed by the universities as an in-kind contribution. Their main responsibility will be to develop and administer credit-bearing college courses through which the services provided by the otherwise noncompensated students will be directed. Students will also be under the direction of a professional. The university coordinators will assure control as to the quality of the services provided to the client.

The services of other professors and key community representatives will be utilized after the program is in operation. They will be used to lead informal seminars on consumer education topics and will represent such departments as economics, marketing, sociology, and business law. These topics will be based on requests from the community.

Other required personnel will include a secretary to the executive director. (Please refer to Section C of the Appendix for a more complete job description for the secretarial position.)

V. BUDGET

The estimated annual costs of operation of the AAS-MD are outlined in the schedule on the following page. In-kind figures refer to the value of donated volunteer time, equipment, and supplies. Professional volunteer time has been valued by for-profit accounting firms in the Detroit Metropolitan area as equal to $35-$50/hour. This rate varies relative to professional criteria, so a weighted average of $35/hour shall be employed. These same local accounting firms have estimated the worth of one hour of donated student time to be equal to $13-$20/hour depending on training and experience. A value of $15/hour will be employed in value estimations.

As you can see from Section A of the Appendix there are similar groups throughout the country. These groups have received monies from the Office of Economic Opportunity (OEO), large national foundations, and community foundations.

We hope to have a significant percentage of our second year budget provided by the accounting profession. (Please refer to Section G of the Appendix.) With the recent formation of the National Association of Accountants for the Public Interest (NAAPI) we have been offered some funds (on a matching basis) for the second year. The matching funds should come from over 200 accounting firms in the metropolitan area as their contribution to public interest accounting in Detroit. NAAPI has offered to assist us in obtaining this broad-based support.

45

THE ACCOUNTING AID SOCIETY OF METROPOLITAN DETROIT

ESTIMATED COSTS

First Year of Operation

OPERATING COSTS	CASH	IN-KIND
Professionals:		
Executive Director	$25,000	
Secretary-Office Manager	7,800	
Fringe Benefits	2,200	
	$35,000	
Consultant Services:		
Professionals		$ 70,000
College Senior Accounting		
and Business Students		70,000
University Coordinators (6)		15,000
		$155,000
Office and Equipment:		
Office Space (1,500 square feet)		$ 2,000
Maintenance	$ 100	
Reproduction Services		700
Telephone	600	
Utilities	500	
	$ 1,200	$ 2,700
Consumable Supplies:		
Pamphlets	$ 300	
Posters	100	
Forms Used in Operation	400	
Office Supplies	400	$ 400
	$ 1,200	$ 400
Other:		
Audit		$ 2,500
Travel Costs (5,000 miles		
@ 12¢/mile	$ 600	
Insurance and Bonding		
Personal Liability Insurance	200	
Fire and Liability Insurance	500	
Postage	400	
Miscellaneous	1,000	
	$ 2,700	$ 2,500
TOTAL OPERATING COSTS	$40,100	$160,600

SHORT-TERM MINORITY
COMMUNITY LEADERSHIP TRAINING

A proposal to the
Marla Friedman Foundation
submitted by
Robbins College

TABLE OF CONTENTS

SHORT-TERM MINORITY COMMUNITY LEADERSHIP TRAINING

NEED

Modern man is in quest for community. This quest is due mainly to a self-worth, identity crisis. It is inclusive of a search for moral certainty, integration of the individual, status, membership, identification, leadership, continuity; in essence, social community.

Whether it involves any one of the larger inner cities or an industrialized suburb or a less densely populated rural area, the quest for community springs from some of the powerful needs of human nature--namely, the need for recognition, security, intimacy, and adventure. Without these needs being satisfied, no amount of material welfare will serve to arrest the developing sense of alienation in our society and the mounting preoccupation with the imperatives of community. It is precisely this issue--the mounting preoccupation with the imperatives of community--that has produced the greatest incentive for the development of a community education program at Robbins College.

The community education program at Robbins College recognizes the basic philosophical assumption of community education as a means whereby individuals to be served by the governmental, educational, and social services establishment have a basic right to active participation in all aspects of these processes. However, the effectiveness of the communities' ability to exercise participation in this type of relationship is not only adversely affected, but also undermined, by an organizational phenomenon--bureaucracy--and by psychological factors such as attitudes, opinions, and prejudices. The community member feels powerless and alienated because much of the contemporary sense of the impersonality of society comes from the impresonality of these organizational bureaucracies. Alienation persists where family, local community, church, and the whole network of interpersonal relationships have ceased to play a determining role in our institutional system of mutual aid, welfare, education, recreation, and economic production and distribution.

Edmond, Maryland, a city in Walker County served by Robbins College, is no different from any other industrial suburban area that has undergone rapid transition from an agrarian community of minority migrant farm workers to an urbanized one. A sense of disorganization, insecurity, instability, and alienation characterizes the feelings of most such community members, but especially minority community members (Asian, Afro-American, Chicano, and Native American), who tend to be relegated to status and positions outside the mainstream of the dominant society. Where there is a sense of isolation among majority group community members, there is an additional sense of isolation among minority group community members. Where there is a need to belong among mainstream community members, minorities' sense of belonging is even more fragile. Where it is difficult for majority group members to navigate the bureaucratic system, minority group members face the same problems as the other members as well as additional problems that result from their minority status.

The most currently available census data for the Edmond community reflect a total population of 101,731. A racial/ethnic breakdown shows 84,015 (82%) Caucasian; 7,050 (7%) Hispanic; 5,072 (5%) Asian; 1,958 (2%) Afro-American; 390 (1%) American Indian; 2,327 (2%) other. (See Attachment A.) One of the big factors that keep these community members outside the mainstream of the community is scarcity of individuals with the leadership skills that would enable these segments of the community to work as equal partners in the problem-solving, decision-making processes. This proposal seeks to implement a pilot short-term training program at the community college level that would provide the necessary conceptual, technical, and human skills for the individual community member in general and the minority group community member in particular.

Community education would offer the city of Edmond a dynamic and comprehensive approach to community problem solving that could pervade all segments of educational, health, social, and cultural programming by directing the thrust of each toward needs of the community. Robbins sees its primary function as a catalytic agent providing knowledge and leadership skills to mobilize community resources in identifying and solving community problems. The marshaling of these community resources (community members and institutions under the auspices of a well-developed community education program would help systems--education, social services, and government--and wise use of community resources. Robbins College is in a unique position to provide and promote the quality of leadership necessary to meet this challenge.

In the initial stages of planning, the Robbins College Community Education Program identified 38 community leaders including indigenous leaders, community school administrators, a Walker County Department of Community Education administrator, and social service administrators and employees. A luncheon was held with the Robbins College staff and the 38 community leaders where an informal needs assessment was conducted revealing the following needs. The order in which the identified needs appear does not necessarily reflect their order of importance.

- Group leadership (facilitative leadership training)
- Followership skills
- Setting of goals and objectives
- Problem-solving skills
- Organizational skills (self and community)
- Political awareness
- Communication skills
- Inter/Cross-cultural communication
- Interpersonal relations

- Public relations skills
- Recruitment skills
- Training skills
- Public speaking skills
- Fund-raising skills
- Agency awareness (interagency coordination)
- Recordkeeping/bookkeeping skills
- Grant-writing skills
- Working relationships with CETA
- Audio-visual skills
- Protocol (chain of command)

This team of Robbins College staff members and community leaders recognizes the potential of developing for the Walker community a program that can "create better opportunity for the individual to exercise his full human potential through using his rights of citizenship and thereby contribute to expanding opportunities for others and the community as a whole." If community education is to help bring the quality of life of community members to an optimum level, individualism must be balanced with a sense of membership--strong community awareness, commitment, and involvement. Robbins College can make a significant contribution toward reinforcing the worth of the Walker community member in ways that will enable him to function effectively in his community, toward supporting true partnership between the individual and community, and in developing and encouraging facilitative, indigenous leadership that provides for continuity even where there is change in headship and recognition of the individual.

This project will provide a pilot program to promote cultural pluralism, interagency cooperation, plurality of association by community members with agencies (utilization of all community resources), and fulfillment of the basic human needs--recognition, security, intimacy, and adventure--through community awareness, commitment, and involvement.

PURPOSE

The primary purpose of this project will be to implement short-term learning opportunities designed specifically to assist the minority community in developing facilitative leadership skills necessary to understand and cope with the governmental, educational, and social service bureaucracy and the prevalent attitudes, opinions, and prejudices of the dominant culture. In addition, the project will create opportunities for men and women, regardless of age, ethnicity, educational background, or economic status, to assume more functional and psychological significance in their community.

GOALS

This project has two major goals and fifteen specific objectives. They are as follows:

I. To provide short-term training in conceptual, technical, and human skills in order to strengthen minority leadership and to promote active participation among members outside mainstream society which will enhance the viability of the community.

Objectives

1. To develop an awareness of political, social, legal, and economic dynamics of community governance and operation.

2. To provide short-term training that will develop an awareness of the organizational theory that underlies traditional bureaucratic systems.

3. To develop an awareness of how the community functions as a curriculum resource.

4. To provide short-term training that will develop skills in organizing to effectively use political, social, legal, and economic leverage.

5. To provide short-term training that will develop skills in how to work with bureaucratic agencies, how to serve on community boards and councils such as boards of education and agency councils, and how to identify community goals and objectives.

6. To provide short-term training that will develop skills in organizational basics and time management.

7. To provide short-term training that will develop skills in how to utilize the community school as a planning center.

8. To provide short-term training that will develop communication skills allowing for community advocacy and for the re-resolution of community conflicts.

9. To provide leadership training that will enhance self-esteem through the recognition of the individual's knowledge and skills as a resource for community improvement.

10. To provide experience in community advocacy.

11. To provide experience in creating, facilitating, and sustaining community-social agency dialogue.

12. To provide short-term training that will emphasize the importance of utilizing minority people in the process of identifying and solving educational problems.

II. To strengthen ties between the community college, the local community school programs, service agencies, the community at large, and minority community members through increased inter-action in identifying their respective needs and responsibil-ities to each other's growth and development.

Objectives

1. To disseminate information that would facilitate a greater community use of the community support resources at the college, e.g., library resources, program and educational consultants, media resources, and instructional resources-- lectures, workshops and course work.

2. To provide opportunities for applying concepts, strategies, and evaluation techniques in explaining and critiquing com-munity agency practices, policies, and programs.

3. To train program participants in understanding and imple-menting the concept of collaboration of resources within the community.

STAFFING

Project Director

The project director will be responsible for the fiscal integrity of the project and provide administrative directions for implementation of the project.

Project Coordinator

The project coordinator will facilitate the development and delivery of the workshops. In addition, the project coordinator will serve as the liaison between the project staff and the community education advisory council keeping all participants apprised of the progress of the project and coor-dinating the project staff and the council. The project coordinator will work closely with the three major task groups of the community council to coordinate their operations. (See the three major task groups of Community Council under Phase I.)

Community Education Advisory Council

A community council composed of interested community persons (special emphasis on minority group community member recruitment), community education practitioners, representatives from the Walker and Francis Community Education Center, and community service agencies will be asked to assist with the implementation of the program in conjunction with the Robbins project staff.

The team will consist of persons with interest and/or expertise in the following areas: community education and facilitative leadership, community power structure (formal and informal), formation and facilitation of task force groups, development of out-reach function (outreach from the college to grassroots constituency), and modular and multimedia instruction.

The community council will be a working council composed of three task force groups to work on such areas as outreach, needs assessment, instructional packaging, and evaluation.

Project Staff

The Robbins College project staff will consist of the intercultural studies division dean, who will be the community education project director; community education project coordinator (to be determined); coordinator of the Community Education and Experience Center (project advisor); existing college faculty to be utilized for delivery of workshops; and a part-time secretarial assistant. This staff, with the assistance of the community education advisory council (also referred to as community council), shall implement the training and provide continuity and expertise for the total program.

PROCEDURE

The project will be conducted in four phases (see Attachment B.) These are as follows.

Phase I

Phase I of operations will be initiated during the first month in three stages. The stages are as follows:

1. Identify and hire community education project coordinator. (This is the only position open for selection.)

2. Orient staff and council to the goals and objectives of the project.

3. Form the three major task groups referred to collectively as the task force. (See Attachment C.) The task groups are:

   a. Outreach task group

      This task group is to be composed of minority group members whose function is to identify members for participation, to act as a liaison to minority community self-help organizations, and to conduct minority members needs assessment.

b. Training task group

This group shall be responsible for evaluating the impact of the program.

Phase II

In Phase II of operations, beginning in the second month, the outreach task group will develop a contact schedule. The contact list will enumerate indigenous community leaders, formal and informal social service organizations, community education practitioners and administrators, and interested teachers and principals in Walker County. Additionally, the outreach team will provide a contact schedule to the project staff. The outreach task group shall begin immediate contact in conjunction with the project coordinator. The function of these contacts will be twofold: 1) To apprise community members (especially minority group members) of the community education project underway at Robbins, and 2) To generate enthusiasm for the project (i.e., energize the community to become actively involved in community education at Robbins).

Upon completion of the contact schedule, which shall not exceed one week (a preliminary contact list has already been developed and used by the project director), the outreach team shall conduct a further and more extensive needs assessment, especially on the needs of minority group members as related to community leadership. Contact will be made with a variety of community self-help organizations to establish the training needs. This team along with the project coordinator shall prepare a progress report of contacts made; general receptivity of the community, especially that of minority group members; and the outcome of the needs assessment compared with the initial needs assessment outlined earlier in this proposal.

This progress report shall be submitted by the outreach task groups and the project coordinator at an all-day conference of the project staff, community council, and training task group to be arranged at the end of the first month and to be conducted at the end of the second month. The first portion of the conference shall include submission of the progress report, perusal, and extensive discussion of the content described earlier. The second half of the conference shall be focused on identifying training objectives and modules to be utilized to meet those objectives.

Phase III

The outreach function shall continue by the outreach task group, and additional contacts will be made with minority community self-help organizations and additional minority community members.

Actual delivery of the community education program will commence at the beginning of the third month and continue through the eleventh month of the project. During this phase, 12 workshops shall be conducted with a minimum of 30 community members and agency people at each workshop. Each workshop will be four hours in duration, providing 48 total hours of instruction. The following list consists of potential topics for the training workshops. (See description of each in Attachment D.)

- Introduction to Community Education

- Community Planning and Organizing

- Cross-cultural Communication

- Citizen Participation and Institutional Behavior

- Human Resource Development

- Community Program Development and Evaluation

- Community Fund Raising

- Community Council and Board Training

- Home-School Community Relations

It is expected that a minimum of 360 community people can be reached by this incentive package. Existing college faculty as well as community and agency representatives will be utilized to deliver the educational program. Since the viability of the program will depend upon the receptivity of participating community members to this program package, every effort will be made to secure outstanding workshop facilitators with expertise in these areas.

Phase IV

In addition to the ongoing formative evaluation process, the project staff in conjunction with the community council, which includes the task force, will conduct a summative evaluation utilizing input from program participants and an external consultant from Francis State University Center for Community Education. This evaluation will be used to determine the program goals and priorities for the succeeding year, and it will take place during the twelfth month at a two-day evaluation session.

EVALUATION

The evaluation of this project will be based on the goals and objectives articulated at the onset of the project. A comprehensive evaluation will involve the following components:

1. The congruency of goals and objectives with the training design

and instructional materials

2. Program management

3. Staff performance

4. Rate of community participation

5. Review of participants' evaluations

Formative evaluation will be employed by the project staff and community council throughout the entire project. Feedback from progress reports will provide information for modifying procedures, as necessary, during implementation of the project. Summative project evaluation will be conducted by the evaluation task group. This team will review the total project and provide a comprehensive written evaluation to the project staff and community council upon completion of the project. (See Attachment C for evaluation team members.)

Robbins College is committed to expanding this project to other areas of Walker County in succeeding years. The evaluation will be used to modify, as necessary, the goals and objectives as well as the implementation procedure to insure that the educational program meets the needs of minority community members.

Dissemination

A project monograph documenting the development and implementation will be disseminated to the American Association of Community and Junior Colleges Center for Community Education, and the Maryland Centers for Community Education. In addition, Robbins College will conduct a one-day information-sharing conference for other community colleges in the area. This conference will be conducted in association with the 1987 Maryland Community and Junior College Association conference.

Proposed Budget

	Marla Friedman Foundation	Robbins College	Total
Project Director (10%)		2,900	2,900
Project Coordinator (1/2 time: Col. II, 3)	8,600		8,600
Clerical Assistant (1/2 time: R29, 3)	5,185		5,185
Fringe Benefits		3,139	3,139
Workshop Facilitators		1,300	1,300
Instructional Materials	1,200		1,200
Travel (Local)	500		500
Other			
Consultants	500		500
Supplies	300		300
Printing	700		700
Postage	200		200
Indirect Costs (24%)	1,375	2,750	4,125
Total	$18,560	$10,069	$28,649

Budget Narrative

Project Director: The project director is the college's administrator for the Division of Intercultural Studies. He will have administrative and fiscal reponsibility for the project at no cost to the grant.

Project Coordinator: (To be determined) The project coordinator will have full responsibility for facilitating the accomplishment of project objectives. This position will be part-time with the cost charged directly to the grant.

Clerical Assistant: (To be determined) The clerical assistant will provide clerical support services to the project director, project coordinator, community education advisory council, and the project staff. This position will be part-time with the cost charged directly to the grant.

Fringe Benefits: Employees are provided income protection insurance, complete health, dental, and vision care, and life insurance.

Workshop Facilitators: Robbins College will provide a minimum of two workshop facilitators for each of the 12 training sessions. Those facilitators will be faculty members with the expertise to deliver the instructional program modules or to work with consultants in the delivery of modules.

Travel: Local travel for project director and coordinator-14¢/mile.

Consultant: $100.00/day for possible special program consultant and/or consultant for project evaluation.

Indirect Cost: 24% indirect cost rate covers space, utilities, phone, office equipment, etc. 8% of the overhead charged to grant, 16% in-kind match by Robbins College.

Education

ADULT LITERACY

HOW TO HELP GROW A READER

A Proposal to the
Meyerhoff Foundation
from
Kansas Junior College
Pleasantville, Kansas

Need for Project

Pleasantville has a higher rate of functional illiteracy than does the state or the nation. There are approximately 15,500 women between the ages of 18 and 39 who have no more than an eighth-grade education. Most of these women are mothers of young children or could be mothers of children in the not-too-distant future. Moreover, most of these women lack the understanding and concise information they need in order to help afford their babies and pre-school children a better opportunity for later success in reading when these children begin school.

To magnify the problem even further, there are additionally thousands of women in Pleasantville with an education above the eighth grade who also do not have the knowledge available to them to help their children develop necessary skills. The goal of this project would be to provide women with what they need to know in order to give their children the maximum opportunity for later success in reading when these children begin school.

Description of Project

Approximately seventeen percent of the women in Drake County between the ages of 18 and 39 have no more than an eighth-grade education. This target population of approximately 15,500 women would be made aware of the availability of a source of information respecting the pre-reading development of their children. The following media would be utilized to publicize the information availability:

1. Project director being interviewed on public and commercial television "talk" shows.

2. Project director being interviewed on the college's radio program.

3. College press releases to the local print media.

4. Public service announcements on area radio and television stations.

5. Posters placed in area shopping centers, the Youth Museum, public libraries, and the college's Center for the Continuing Education of Women.

The objectives of the counseling and instructional aspects of this project would be as follows:

1. To provide mothers and other interested women with a clear understanding of what reading is.

2. To make mothers and other interested women aware of the reading readiness skills that their children will need to develop before they can successfully learn to read.

67

3. To provide mothers and interested women with some suggestions for pre-reading activities and ways they can aid reading growth of their pre-school children.

4. To give mothers and other interested women the answers to questions that are often asked about reading in regard to the pre-school child.

5. To give mothers an opportunity to increase their self-concepts and their feelings of value as parents.

The project would be housed at the Brown Campus of the Kansas Junior College (KJC). This campus is the most centrally-located of the three KJC campuses. It is easily accessible by bus or car. This campus is also the most accessible for the central-city women who have the least education and who have the greatest dependency on public bus transportation of all women in Pleasantville.

A counseling center would provide the following services:

1. Counseling by the project director (a reading specialist who is also certified in early childhood educations) or the parent/child counselor for any woman with concerns and questions regarding her child's pre-reading development.

2. Practical literature including the "How to Help Grow a Reader" booklet that women can take home with them to guide them in providing their children with pre-reading activities.

3. A class that meets once a week for six weeks. This unique class would consist of interested women, mothers, and their children. The women would be taught to work with children on pre-reading activities and skills in a laboratory setting.

In addition, one class will be continually taught from January through July by the project director at each of the other two campuses of KJC. This will allow an interested woman the opportunity to choose the most convenient of the three different locations to enroll. Each class would meet once a week for six weeks. Therefore, twenty classes would be taught with a combined enrollment of a minimum of 500 women. During each class while the project director would be instructing the women respecting a given pre-reading activity, the parent/child counselor would be meeting with the children who would be engaged in an activity related to that which their mothers are studying. After the women have conceptualized the activity, they would join the children for completion of the activity.

In order to measure the effectiveness of the class activities and the degree of awareness-gain experienced by each participating woman, a unique survey instrument would be utilized. This survey instrument would be developed by the project director and a professor of reading from the University of South Kansas (USK). The draft survey instrument would be reviewed for relevance by four professors of reading and by three professors of early childhood education from Adamson College, University of Kansas, USK, and KJC. The final survey instrument draft would reflect modifications suggested by the seven reviewers. The survey instrument would be administered as a pre- and post-test to each participating woman for the purpose of measuring her knowledge of pre-reading development and the importance of developing pre-reading skills before entering school. The difference in the mean gain score would indicate the degree of enhanced awareness acquired by each participating woman. A test of significance (e.g., Scheffe) would be used to locate specific significant differences on survey items.

The activities constituting this project would occur as follows:

1.	Develop survey instrument	September - November
2.	Project publicity	Ongoing
3.	Counseling center operational for a minimum of twenty-five hours per week	December - August
4.	Twenty classes of instruction	January - July
5.	Project summary report written and disseminated	August

Dissemination of Results

The results of this project would be promulgated via the distribution of the project summary reports to pre-school reading educators. The names of these educators will be gleaned from the membership of the following professional organizations: International Reading Association, National Association for Education of Young Children, Kansas State Reading Council, and Kansas Association for Children Under Six.

Moreover, the project director would present an overview of the project and results to date at the following conferences:

Kansas State Reading Council (October in Montgomery, Kansas)
Kansas Association for Children Under Six (October in Pleasantville, Kansas)
National Association for Education of Young Children (November in Chicago, Illinois)
International Reading Association (May in Houston, Texas)

Project Budget - 12 months

1. External Funding Source Component

   A. Staff

      1) Project Director $18,175

      2) Parent-Child Coordinator
           (9 months - December thru August)   10,425

      3) Secretary   5,250

      4) Fringe Benefits (social security, retirement,
           medical and life insurance)   3,131

   B. Travel

      1) Travel to Conferences

           a. International Reading Association - Houston, Texas

           b. National Association for Education of Young Children -
              Chicago, Illinois

           c. Kansas State Reading Conference - Montgomery, Kansas

           d. Airfare: $356   Car: $63 Per diem: $375   794

      2) Travel local - 4,000 miles at 14¢/mile   560

   C. Other

      1) Educational Materials   2,420

      2) Data Analysis   250

      3) Printing

           a. 1,000 project summary reports @ 75¢/report   750

           b. 2,500 "How to Help Grow a Reader" booklets   750

                                               $42,505

II. Kansas Junior College's Contribution

    A. Telephone (installation, rental, and
        long distance) $1,325

    B. Postage   350

                                          1,675

    In addition, the college would provide office space and furnishings for the project director, parent/child counselor, and project secretary.

III. Total Project Budget $44,180

COOPERATIVE EDUCATION PROGRAM

A Proposal

from

Brandon College

TABLE OF CONTENTS

PHILOSOPHY AND INSTITUTIONAL COMMITMENT

The administration and staff at Brandon College propose the implementation of a cooperative education program designed to strengthen the educational background of students by creating a meaningful linkage between academic studies and practical work experience. A cooperative education program relates directly to Brandon College's mission to provide students with a variety of meaningful educational experiences in a diversity of learning environments. The college fully recognizes the value of meaningful cooperative work experiences as they relate to education. A cooperative education program provides an appropriate partnership in education--one that relates the student, employer, and faculty member in the process of enriching the student's knowledge and experience. The college's commitment to this philosophy of cooperative education is demonstrated by the development of the Insight Program. Insight provides students with the academic credits for general education requirements in the School of University Transfer Studies as well as a career exploration opportunity at one of a variety of locations off campus. This proposal seeks federal support to create a formal cooperative education program based on Brandon's experience with the Insight Program, and to make the cooperative education program available to a larger number of students and academic disciplines.

ORIGINS AND SUPPORT OF COOPERATIVE EDUCATION

The existing career exploration component in the Insight Program will be converted to the cooperative mode. This will allow students to test various work experiences and academic interests before finalizing a career choice, to earn necessary funds to continue formal education, and to gain college credits for work experience which adds relevance to the classroom experience. Academic credit has been recognized in the past for career exploration; an increase in credit is anticipated for those students involved in a cooperative education experience.

The Insight Program, which was developed by the faculty, has continued to receive solid budget and moral support from the president of Brandon College, from the vice president for academic affairs, from the dean of the School of University Transfer Studies, and from the dean of the School of Career Education. This support will continue for the cooperative education program (see Appendix A).

The interest in the cooperative education concept comes from not only the administration and faculty but also from students and employers. Brandon has had a continuing demand from employers in the college's district to extend the program to cooperative education (see Appendix B). Reception to the program from students and support from the faculty have been high (see Appendix C). As a result of this interest, the vice president of academic affairs formed a steering committee comprised of administrators and faculty members to consider options for cooperative education. Ad hoc subcommittees included administrators, faculty, students, and employers. The committees held numerous meetings over the past two years to discuss the merits and problems of initiating a cooperative education program. As a result of these meetings, and with the already existing institutional commitment to the concept of cooperative education, Brandon's president, vice president of academic affairs, and deans are prepared to cooperate with pragmatic aspects by supporting a director and the faculty in an interdisciplinary approach to insure that both academic studies and the work experience are more meaningful to the students. Thomas Woodson, professor of cooperative education at Carolyn College, and John Allen, dean of cooperative education at Johnson College, were used as consultants in this planning stage (See Appendix D).

PROGRAM STATUS

The following planning procedures have been completed in the year 1977-78 in order to prepare for the implementation of the cooperative education program at Brandon College. The committee has:

1. Designated the institutional staff responsible for coordinating the respective disciplines. This staff has organized the general education curriculum for students to interrelate with career exploration experiences.

2. Surveyed district employers for industrial and business training sites. More than 400 employers have agreed to participate as employers of students in the cooperative education program (see Appendix E). This would expand the range of specific opportunities to include those in business, industry, education, and social services occupations.

3. Identified two cooperative education consultants to administer staff in-service training programs in cooperation with the project director. These consultants are Professor Thomas Woodson and Dean John Allen (see Appendix D).

4. Developed selected materials for use in job placements, accounting systems, and job evaluations by students, employers, supervisors, and faculty advisors (see Appendix F).

5. Articulated a philosophy of cooperative education that includes a commitment on the part of the college administration and instructional staffs to provide students with not only academic opportunities in a classroom environment but also the opportunity to gather on-the-job training in off-campus learning environments. This written philosophy will continue to be refined as the college moves into successive phases of a cooperative education program.

6. Arranged curriculum revision to accommodate the cooperative education students' new schedules each semester, allowing for aca-

demic instruction to alternate with work cycles. Students
will spend a minimum of two semesters in the cooperative
education program. The work experience and the academic
study will operate on a parallel mode. There is provision
for a weekly seminar in which work experiences and problems are discussed on campus with a college counselor,
the program director, and the specific curriculum coordinator of students' programs.

7. Established a system for the visitation of students in
    off-campus career placements to promote the application
    of academic theory to the student's work experience.

8. Established a work contract that defines the relationship
    between the student, the employer, and the supervisor.
    This contract contains competency statements that are the
    substance of the mid-term and final evaluation of the stu-
    dent (see Appendix G). Academic credit has been recognized
    in the past for work experience. It is anticipated that
    formal amounts and types of credits will be established as
    the cooperative education experience is approved by both
    the college and its accrediting agency.

9. Arranged a formal recordkeeping system. There is internal
    departmental tracking as well as institutional recordkeep-
    ing through the formal registration procedures. This ac-
    countability system will keep track of each student's status,
    attendance periods, and work periods.

10. Established a working relationship with the Brandon College
    Placement Office. The placement office has on file over
    400 requests from employers who are willing to make avail-
    able their resources for cooperative education students.

11. Altered the academic calendar to accommodate the parallel
    mode of career exploration for students in the majority
    of disciplines selected for the Insight Program. These
    include: rhetoric, speech, humanities, psychology, and
    philosophy. This unique combination of liberal arts gen-
    eral education courses in combination with career explora-
    tion will be maintained and modified as Brandon develops
    its cooperative education program.

SPECIFIC OBJECTIVES OF PROPOSED COOPERATIVE EDUCATION PROGRAM

With such strong institutional, community, and student interest and support, FY 1979 would be an ideal time for Brandon to establish its cooperative education program as a viable program which will ultimately be able to
support itself through the resulting new enrollment. This proposal seeks
financial support to improve and expand its present offerings in the fol-

lowing manner:

- To establish a formal cooperative education office and hire a director. The college is currently in a building program and has allocated prime space in its new Community Career Center for the cooperative education offices, large class-room areas, and seminar rooms. This location will be both accessible and flexible (see Appendix H).

- To recruit 100 students for the cooperative education program (increasing students per annum). The cooperative education director, in conjunction with the counselor, placement person-nel, and appropriate faculty members, will be responsible for recruiting prospective cooperative education students.

- To prepare and disseminate appropriate literature to students, administration, faculty, and industry. The cooperative education director will develop brochures, newsletters, and related com-munications to promote the program.

- To strengthen existing relationships and build new ones be-tween the college and industry - increasing by 50 new alter-nating jobs per annum. The counselor/coordinator will pro-vide for continued growth in the number and quality of coop-erative education job experiences. This person will also act as job counselor to the students and as a liaison between the students and industry.

- To provide career development skills through work experience and participation in classroom training. Faculty members will assist in relating the work experience to classroom ex-perience to help the students become aware of the educational benefits of their work experience.

- To provide counseling for students enrolled in the cooperative education program. The counselor/coordinator will provide counseling for students enrolled in the cooperative education program and serve as liaison between the students and support services offered by the college.

- To develop new instruments to evaluate the cooperative educa-tion program. The cooperative education director will be re-sponsible for developing evaluation instruments to complement those now used in the Insight Program.

- To develop an advisory committee including administration, faculty, students, and employers. The cooperative education director will form an advisory committee to provide assis-tance to the program. The director will be made aware of the status of community college students in the business world.

The committee will further provide assistance to the program through recommendations on topics related to curriculum changes or industry-related problems.

- To provide support services such as career and academic counseling and including testing and placement (see Appendix I).

- To develop in-service for faculty and to provide time for cooperative education conferences.

- To prepare a handbook for cooperative education.

- To continue to provide input to the college's curriculum and calendar committees to insure that they address the needs of the cooperative education students.

- To evaluate the cooperative education program at the completion of the 1979-80 school year.

It is the college's intent to seek funding to develop a staff responsible for the cooperative education program (see Appendix J for job descriptions). The staff will consist of:

Project Director
Cooperative Education Director
Faculty Cooperative Education Coordinators (5)
Cooperative Education Coordinator/Job Developer
Project Secretary
Part-time Counselors (2)
Consultants (2)

EVALUATION PROCEDURES

The evaluation of the cooperative education program is crucial to its success. Brandon College will use a three-pronged approach to evaluation. This will include an in-house evaluation, an outside independent evaluation, and a cost-effective evaluation of the program. Faculty, students, employers, and administrators will provide an ongoing inside evaluation on a regular basis (quarterly). Outside independent evaluators, Professor Thomas Woodson and Dean John Allen (see Appendix D), specialists in cooperative education, will be used to evaluate the program in an effort to gain specific and constructive criticism. They will provide a minimum of two evaluations--one at three months into the program and a final review of the program at the end of the year.

The director of the cooperative education program, vice president for academic affairs, and vice president-business management will determine the cost effectiveness of each class and of the program as a whole, and the benefit estimates on the part of students completing the program. Existing evaluation forms will be modified to accommodate the cooperative education program. The intent of the evaluation is to understand better the impact of our cooperative education program and to provide Brandon with information which will help to continue to expand the program in the directions best able to serve the students and the community at large.

FUTURE DIRECTIONS

With the support of the U.S. Office of Education to initiate Brandon College's cooperative education program, it is felt that gradually the institution will be more supportive of the academic viability of this program and will commit further resources to its support. Up to this time, staff support has been apparent. With continuing administrative and faculty support, and student interest, it is anticipated that this program will double in enrollment and job placements by the end of five years. The college is convinced that the cooperative education program will indeed enrich and extend educational opportunities for the Brandon students enrolled in this program, as well as provide them with the necessary employable skills for successful futures.

NEH CONSULTANT
HUMANITIES FOR CAREER EDUCATION
submitted by
WHITNER COLLEGE

TABLE OF CONTENTS

Summary

Whitner College, a public community college and technical institute, was founded 14 years ago to serve over 400,000 residents in 23 communities in the western suburbs of Salem, New Jersey. The curriculum trends of the past few years provided a climate which necessitated reassessment by the humanities department relative to its role in the mission of the college. As a result of faculty and student surveys, the humanities department determined that it could best fulfill the mission of the college by expanding humanities curricula to meet the needs of vocational/technology students.

The purpose of this consultancy would be to:

1. Develop realistic plans for integrating the humanities with technical education curricula;

2. Review and recommend changes in existing curricula that will be more beneficial to technology students; and

3. Evaluate the scope of the proposed course for technology students, determine its relevance, and suggest materials, resources, and instructional techniques.

Institutional Background

Whitner College, a publicly supported community college and technical institute, is recognized for the high quality and broad spectrum of its educational programs and services. Now in its fourteenth year of operation, the college serves a variety of students through its various programs in the divisions of university transfer studies, career education, and school of continuing education.

Located in the western suburbs of Salem, New Jersey, Whitner serves 23 communities in a 63 square mile area with over 400,000 residents. (See Appendix A.) The 25,000 full-time and part-time students participate in an array of educational programs which include over 100 career programs, 14 university transfer majors, and numerous continuing education programs. Whitner College is fully accredited as a two-year, degree granting institution by the Northeastern Association of Schools and Colleges and has additional accreditation from other pertinent professional organizations. The excellence of the college's programs is demonstrated by the success of its graduates in career fields and in the continued academic achievement of its university transfer graduates. Whitner College has an open door admission policy. The average ACT score is 17. There are no faculty rankings, and all faculty are classified as instructors. The social science division, which includes the humanities department, has 28 full-time faculty (see Appendix B) who are dedicated to teaching, providing instruction which is both intensive and comprehensive.

Discussion of the Problem

The continuing assaults of inflation, the decline in enrollment, the depressed job market, and the growing trend toward vocationalism have influenced much of the curriculum development at the community college level. While many departments are experiencing general declines as a result of these phenomena, the humanities department has been hardest hit. In an attempt to manage this decline, the humanities department surveyed the career education division to determine the extent to which both groups shared similar percepts and concerns. (See Appendix C.) It was determined that both faculties did indeed feel the need for improved student preparation in humanities. The results support additional institutional research which demonstrated student self-awareness of deficiencies in humanities-related skills. The humanities faculty at Whitner College recognized its obligation to seriously examine the future of humanities curricula in relation to the preparation of vocational/technology students. An analysis of this issue has led to the conviction that the mission of the humanities department must be re-examined and redefined.

The humanities faculty has proposed and received approval to develop a new course which will be designed for career education students. This offering, Humanities 099, is the outgrowth of the humanities department's evaluation of strengths and weaknesses in the existing curricula and an attempt to address the needs of career education students. Humanities 099 components have been developed to meet the needs of students in allied health and preprofessional services. However, the faculty has been unable to develop a similar component for technology students.

Purpose of Consultancy

The humanities department at Whitner College has agreed upon the need for a consultant who will be able to assist the faculty in the following areas:

1) Develop realistic plans for integrating the humanities with technical education curricula.

2) Review and recommend changes in the existing curricula that will be more beneficial to technology students.

3) Evaluate the scope of the proposed course, Humanities 099, to determine its relevance and to suggest materials, resources, and instructional techniques and approaches to be used.

Desired Consultant Qualifications

We seek a consultant who is familiar with the mission of community colleges and who has expertise in humanities as it relates to technology.

WILLIS COUNTY DROPOUT ASSESSMENT PROJECT

BERNARD COLLEGE

September 24, 1979

Office of the State Employment and Training Council
Department of Natural Resources and Community Development

CONTENTS

WILLIS COUNTY DROPOUT ASSESSMENT PROJECT

I. BASIC PROJECT INFORMATION

A. Service Area--The project will be centered in Willis County. The project will work primarily with local school systems.

B. Target Groups--The project will research the high school dropouts in Willis County and the programs and services being provided to them.

C. Project Beginning and Ending Dates--October 1, 1979 to September 30, 1980.

D. Total Amount of Funds Requested--$48,044

E. Program Description--The major goal of the project is to establish a better service delivery system for dropouts in Willis County through an assessment of the dropout population and an analysis of the programs available to dropouts through CETA-sponsored programs, educational institutions, and social services.

The second goal of the project is to determine the level of linkage between the service agencies, CETA-sponsored programs, and educational institutions and to suggest possible further linkages.

The project will be divided into four parts: 1) assessment, 2) analysis, 3) dissemination, and 4) evaluation. Assessment will be a prime objective during the first four months of the project, although it will extend through its entire life. Analysis will take place during the fifth month of the project and will be facilitated by a visiting consultant. Dissemination will take place during the last six months of the project. Finally, a formal evaluation will take place during the last six weeks of the project.

II. PROJECT OPERATOR'S QUALIFICATIONS

A. Type of Organization--Bernard College is one of the 58 community colleges in the state. The college is located in Willis County, with the main campus in Jamestown. Bernard College is a public institution funded by Willis County and the state.

B. Previous Experience--Bernard College offers a variety of technical and vocational programs. Over the past seven years it has operated three service programs of the employment and training nature. These programs consisted of an employment counseling and referral project operated in cooperation with a local model cities program, a state-funded human resources development program, and a federally funded CETA project.

II. PROJECT OPERATOR'S QUALIFICATIONS (continued)

B. Previous Experience (continued)

The employment counseling and referral program, which utilized model city funds, existed for a period of approximately 20 months. During this period of time the college successfully provided counseling and employment referrals to the disadvantaged residents of the City of Jamestown.

Bernard College, utilizing the staff of its employment counseling and referral program, applied for and received funds to operate a state-funded human resources development program through the department of community colleges. This program has been in existence for a period of six years. During this six-year period the college has served over 800 residents in Willis County. Services provided include employment counseling, personal counseling, classroom instruction, job placement, and follow-up. The recipients of these services have primarily been the unemployed, underemployed, and disadvantaged residents of the county. The purpose of human resources development is to introduce or to reintroduce individuals to the world of work by providing counseling, classroom training, job placement, and follow-up, which the college's HRD program has successfully done. As a result of these factors, the college will continue to operate its HRD program.

Bernard College has been involved in manpower training for many years. Prior to 1973 the college operated an MDTA program, and since that time it has been very much involved in the Comprehensive Employment and Training Act training programs. Several hundred students have received skills training in many areas as a result of the college's involvement with the CETA program. At this time the college is expanding its training offerings and will add a new service program during 1980 fiscal year.

C. Administrative Structure--The coordinator of the project will report to the director of institutional research.

The citizens of Willis County serve on advisory councils and boards advising instructors and staff in vocational and technical areas.

An advisory council will be established composed of representatives from the educational institutions and social agencies concerned with dropouts in Willis County. The council will consist of 10 members and will concern itself with facilitating the work of the project staff.

D. Statement--A copy of this proposal will be sent to Mr. Aaron Washing-

II. PROJECT OPERATOR'S QUALIFICATIONS (continued)

   D. Statement (continued)

   ton, Manpower Coordinator, The Willis County Manpower Development
   Office.

III. PROGRAM DESCRIPTION

   A. Goals and Objectives

   The dropout assessment project will focus on the following goals:

   1. Assessment of the present level of linkage existing among the
      service agencies, CETA-sponsored programs, and educational
      institutions of Willis County.

   2. Development of a delivery service model that can be used to
      identify potential dropouts and can assist them and those
      already out of school to gain the necessary skills, abilities,
      and confidences needed for success in an academic and/or an
      employment setting.

   Objectives of the project will include:

   1. Identification of the Willis County dropout population, with
      name and point of contact from the county high school rolls and
      student data base.

   2. Creation of an advisory committee composed of representative
      educational, social service, and CETA-sponsored program personnel
      to work with the project staff in planning and implementing
      details of the project.

   3. An investigation of services available to Willis County high
      school youth.

   4. Creation of a "typical" Willis County high school dropout
      profile, using random sampling and statistical techniques.

   The major objectives of the project will be divided into four levels:
   assessment, analysis, dissemination, and evaluation.

   1. Assessment, scheduled for the first four months of the project,
      will be an ongoing process coordinated with evaluation. Within
      Willis County during the 1977-78 school year, 4,674 dropouts
      were reported. The 1976-77 school year report noted 5,069
      additional dropouts. This project will focus on these 9,743
      former students and will:

      a. Identify students, via random sampling, and contact them

III. PROGRAM DESCRIPTION (continued)

A. Goals and Objectives (continued)

personally to obtain biographic, demographic, and academic data from the questionnaires, phone calls, and interviews conducted by the project staff.

b. Concurrently, contact personnel and examine county social service programs, CETA-sponsored programs, and educational opportunities for impact, effectiveness, performance, and future developments.

c. Amass the data for entry into the county's computer system.

2. Analysis of the collected data will be accomplished by statistically computing it for correlation. Assistance for the analysis part of the project will be provided by an outside consultant who will work with the project staff.

3. Dissemination of the project's progress and analyzed data will be accomplished by ten (10) workshops, a printed report, open meetings of all involved parties, and a list of recommendations submitted by the project staff to the county's social service agencies, and to the CETA-sponsored program directors. Information presented will include:

a. Characteristics of the "typical" Willis County dropout, numbers, history, postdropout success.

b. A list of services and opportunities available from the county's service, educational, employment, and CETA-sponsored program agencies for the currently enrolled high school student and his or her dropout counterpart.

c. A developed service delivery system model for the Willis County dropout with suggested linkages.

4. Evaluation of the dropout assessment project will be an ongoing process conducted by the project staff with the assistance of an outside consultant. Formally, evaluation will take place during the last six weeks of the project, with success contingent upon:

a. The formulation of a final written report regarding the characteristics of dropouts in Willis County and the services presently being offered to them.

b. The establishment of a suggested system of coordination and linkage between social services, educational, employment,

III. PROGRAM DESCRIPTION (continued)

A. Goals and Objectives (continued)

and CETA-sponsored program agencies to better serve the dropout population of the county.

B. Job Descriptions

1. Project Director

Working primarily with the director of institutional research at Bernard College and the superintendents of two local educational systems, this person will coordinate with county guidance counselors, employment agency personnel, and CETA-sponsored program staff members in developing the schedule for project activity; in coordinating the identification of data elements and their collection; in determining the method of best contact for identified dropouts; and in disseminating the analyzed data. This person will supervise the project staff and will operate from the Jamestown campus of Bernard College.

2. Secretary

Responsible to the project director, this person will set up files to house data collected; will handle budget for program and expense sheet; will prepare questionnaires, correspondence, and project results for distribution; will share space on the campus of Bernard College with the institutional research and resource development offices; and will work with community agencies handling phone calls, personal visits, and routine correspondence.

C. Linkages and Coordination

The project director will work with various agencies in Willis County including:

1. Department of Social Services

2. Employment Security Commission

3. Youth Services Bureau

4. Educational institutions at the primary, secondary, and post-secondary levels

5. Vocational Rehabilitation Center

6. Mental Health Association

III. PROGRAM DESCRIPTION (continued)

    C. Linkages and Coordination (continued)

        7. Drug Action Council

        8. Bernard College

> Human Resource Development Program
> Adult High School
> Adult Basic Education

        9. Special program oriented to dropouts in two local school systems

        10. Sheltered Workshop

        11. CETA-sponsored agencies

        12. Willis County Native American Association

        13. Various information and referral services

The project will be coordinated by the project director through the established advisory council.

    D. Evaluation

Evaluation of the project will be coordinated by the project director working with the advisory committee members, school superintendents, the director of institutional research at Bernard College and the outside consultant. The ten (10) workshops will provide the feedback necessary to determine progress.

IV. SUITABILITY FOR GOVERNOR'S SPECIAL GRANT FUNDING

    A. Innovation

Very little has been done to assess the service delivery system to dropouts in the state. This project will be innovative in that it will bring together information on this population and the services available to the population. It will also suggest ways that linkages may be created to assist these individuals.

    B. Suitability

This research project will be limited to researching the characteristics of the dropout population and the services presently serving the dropout population. The project is particularly suited to the requirement of the 1 percent linkage money.

IV. SUITABILITY FOR GOVERNOR'S SPECIAL GRANT FUNDING (continued)

B. Suitability (continued)

The developed model should be applicable to other counties through-out the state. Funds are not available locally to support such a research project on linkage.

C. Future Funding

The project has been planned for one year to bring together the data needed for future planning. Other sources of funds will be secured from the regular operating funds as well as federal categorical funds, depending on the findings of this project, to continue serving the needs of dropouts in Willis County.

Science

SELF PACED INDIVIDUALIZED MODULES

ON HUMAN PSYCHOBIOLOGY

PRESENTED BY

CRESTWOOD COLLEGE

TABLE OF CONTENTS

SUMMARY

It is the intent of this project to develop a nontraditional self-paced instruction program on human psychobiology to serve five basic needs: 1) to enhance instructional quality by conveying content on a self-paced basis; 2) to provide a low-cost alternative to laboratory experiments by simulating laboratory experiences; 3) to provide supplemental academic material for students in various allied health curricula; 4) to design a program that could be utilized by other schools unable to buy, house, and maintain laboratory equipment; and 5) to provide accurate specialized information to individuals who are involved in, or are preparing for, careers in gerontology, psychology, psychiatric social work, handicapped education, or other fields dealing with brain-impaired clients. These needs will be addressed by developing 20 individualized modules of approximately one hour duration each. These modules will consist of slide/tape or videotape programs supported by individual student activity worksheets. All scripts will be developed by the project director and will incorporate the most current research available. The scripts will be evaluated by expert consultants in neuropsychology and neurophysiology for accuracy and appropriateness of subject content. The production team will convert the scripts to self-paced instructional modules utilizing an appropriate instructional design model. A two-phased evaluation will be conducted. An evaluation instrument will be used to measure educational effectiveness and aesthetic quality of the media. In addition, a pilot study will be conducted to evaluate the effectiveness of the package under instructional conditions.

NEED

Crestwood College, of the Raritan Valley Community College District, has rapidly emerged as one of the outstanding community colleges in the country. Now in its twenty-first year of operation, Crestwood has established its philosophy of "educational opportunity for all" through a sound balance between classroom instruction and out-of-class activity to meet the needs of students and the community. The college serves a variety of traditional and nontraditional students and offers classes on and off campus, in the day and evening, on Saturday, and via local television.

Located on a 122 acre campus approximately 5 miles south of Edison, Crestwood College serves over 14,000 full-time and continuing education students from six surrounding communities.

Crestwood College is a publicly supported community college that provides the first two years of collegiate education to post high school youths and adults, curricula for students who wish to enter gainful employment at the end of two years of college or less, general education opportunities for adults, and an extensive range of community service programs to meet other educational, cultural, and recreational needs of the people in the service area.

As part of the Raritan Valley Community College District, Crestwood College is a charter member of the League for Innovation in the Community

College. Membership identifies the district and its colleges as institutions committed to experimentation and innovation, evaluation, willingness to share the fruits of its activities, and cooperation with others in the solution of common problems.

The psychology department in the division of social science has nine faculty who teach a full complement of courses for undergraduate transfer and electives. One of the courses now taught is psychobiology. This course focuses upon nervous system processes underlying the behavior of man and animals including (1) anatomical substrates of behavior and consciousness, (2) basic methods of studying behavior and consciousness, and (3) neural mechanisms associated with perception, emotion, motivation, memory, learning, and language.

Most authors of psychobiology texts would agree that their major objective is to describe brain-behavior relationships which have the potential of illuminating aspects of human nervous system processes. Animal surrogates of man have been the principal focus of most physiological psychology texts in large part because only in the last few years has a great deal of human information been accessible, particularly with regard to recent developments in the study of amnesia, agnosia, aphasia, and the biological aspects of psychosis, dementia, and senility. The latter topics are given minimal coverage in most physiological psychology texts surveyed (Morgan, 1965; Grossman, 1967; Thompson, 1967; Butter, 1968; Milner, 1970; Isaacson, et al., 1971; Leukel, 1972; Deagle, 1973; Deutch, 1973; Schwartz, 1973; Beatty, 1975; Gazzaniga, 1975; Teyler, 1975; Bruce, 1976; Hart, 1976), although the trend is reversed in a more recent text (Plotnik & Mollenauer, 1978).

In comparison most works concerning neuropsychology have placed less emphasis upon the more traditional topics of sensory systems, sleep, attention, emotion, and motivation (Luria, 1970, 1976; Eisenson, 1972; Goodglass & Kaplan, 1973; Brown, 1974; Williams, 1974; Gardner, 1975; Knights 1976a, 1976b; Hecaen & Albert, 1976, 1978), with two exceptions (Pribram, 1971 and Watts, 1975). The latter two integrate physiological psychology and neuropsychology but are written for the graduate student.

From this survey it appears that an undergraduate program that distills human findings from psychobiology that include elements of physiological psychology and neuropsychology can provide a comprehensive introduction to psychobiology (see Appendix 2).

At Crestwood College, introduction to psychobiology is taught with a traditional lecture format. It is the intent of this project to develop a nontraditional self-paced instruction (SPI) program with an audiocassette-slide format to serve five basic needs:

1. SPI modules (SPI-M) will enhance the quality of instruction by conveying content on a self-paced basis thus providing the opportunity for clarifying complex concepts from the neurosciences.

2. SPI-M will substitute for a costly electrophysiological laboratory by providing simulated laboratory experience and considerable information.

3. SPI-M will provide a natural link to the paramedical trainee programs offered at Crestwood College such as biomedical instrumentation, emergency medical technology, and radiation therapy.

4. SPI-M will be designed as a complete program and thus can provide for the school that is unable to afford to buy, house, and maintain biomedical instrumentation a laboratory equivalent at a small fraction of the cost.

5. SPI-M will be highly informative to the student who may prepare for a career in a field where brain-impaired patients, psychiatric patients, or geriatric patients are assisted, or for the professionals presently working with such patients.

We shall address each of the five needs in order of presentation.

First, how will SPI-M clarify information and present concepts? The "information explosion" in the neurosciences has produced contributions to the study of the human brain from physiological psychology, neuropsychology, neuroanatomy, psychopharmacology, neurochemistry, neuroradiology, and other disciplines. Presented as single studies the data are difficult to assimilate. Presented as general outlines where the data are primarily drawn from human research the data are more easily grasped. By stressing human psychobiology we can expand the traditional topics of psychobiology to include aphasia, agnosia, amnesia, the biological aspects of psychological problems, dementia, and senility, and studies of other higher processes (see Appendix 3).

The Individual Study Center (ISC) at Crestwood has a team specialized in the development of nontraditional instruction. With skill and dedication complex information can be imparted directly and with precision so that mastery of learning objectives will result. The ISC has a software dispensing service that complements individualized learning and accessibility to materials (see Appendix 4).

Second, SPI-M can provide laboratory-related experience by the following means:

1. Demonstrate aspects of physiology and anatomy through visual exposure. Illustrations in color will be created to detail significant structures in the nervous system and their relationship to behavior. These shall include, for example, neuronal connections, sensory system projections, motor system projections, aspects of the hypothalamus and limbic system relating to mood and memory, and cortical fields which relate to functions of neuropsychological processes, such as language and visuospatial concepts.

2. Simulate experiments, which show in a step-by-step way, the development of hypotheses, methods, results, and conclusions. By utilizing equipment from the Biomedical Instrumentation Program at Crestwood College and from the research laboratories of Buxtons University, it will be possible to demonstrate how electroencephalographic activity is recorded, displayed, and analyzed in the waking and sleeping individual, how averaged evoked potentials are studied, how indices of the autonomic nervous system are measured including blood pressure, heart rate, skin resistance, and skin temperature. In addition, anatomical sections of human brain and radiological indices of normal and damaged brain will be available. Finally, it will be possible to obtain, with appropriate consent, information from brain-damaged patients with disorders of memory, language, and recognition, so that the student has a direct understanding of aspects of brain damage.

3. Application of discoveries in the neurosciences which have relevance to the understanding of the human brain and behavior. For example, with prior permission of Buxtons researchers, it may be possible to document implantation of cochlear prosthetics, specify how sleep disturbances are aided, and how convulsive disturbances are treated by medication. Appropriate consent forms will be used (see Appendix 5).

Third, SPI-M has direct applicability to the 1150 majors at Crestwood College in biology, psychology, paramedical and allied health professions. The biomedical equipment trainee, for example, will learn more of the origin, generation, and clinical significance of selected bioelectrical signals, including EEG and EKG. The emergency medical technology trainee could be more extensively familiarized with sleep, shock, coma, and vital signs. The radiation therapy trainee could learn how brain damage identified by computerized tomography scans produces various alterations of behavior. In addition, speech pathology majors could learn more about the lesions producing aphasia, modes of recovery, and selected therapies. The nursing major could learn how psychobiological studies relate to topics such as sleep, chemotherapy, psychiatric disorders, heroin addiction, and other disorders.

Fourth, SPI-M will be designed to offer a comprehensive five unit course in human psychobiology. A school equipped with appropriate equipment (sound-activated slides or video cassette players) can offer instruction in this field without the costly development of a laboratory. The modular characteristic of SPI enables a school to obtain highly specific information of value to particular health professions. We believe the present SPI-M program will be the first to detail an entire course in human psychobiology.

Finally, individuals enrolled in paraprofessional programs related to mental health and gerontology would be able to utilize the SPI-M program for supplementary academic background on an individual basis. It would be possible for students to utilize specific modules relevant to their needs without having to undertake the complete course.

OVERALL PRODUCTION OBJECTIVES

1. Create a mediated human psychobiology course that is self-paced.
2. Adapt the current lecture material to scripts more appropriate to media presentations.
3. Develop 20 slide-tape programs that present the most current research findings in human psychobiology.
4. Provide simulated lab experiences with equipment commonly used in psychobiological research.
5. Develop two videotapes for those units in which concepts of motion are necessary.
6. Develop an instructor's handbook to aid the teacher of record who is coordinating necessary administration of the self-paced course.
7. Develop a workbook containing directions, activity sheets, and evaluation forms for student participation.

8. Develop a bibliography of supplemental academic materials available.
9. Develop pretests and program evaluation instruments to field test the effectiveness of unit modules on students.

PROJECT AND PROGRAM OBJECTIVES

The project will help to introduce students to currently important scientific developments in human psychobiology through a series of 20 modules. Illustrated below are 20 modules in five separate units that correspond to the five academic units of the class.

Human Psychobiology

I. The Matter of Mind
   1. Origins of Man
   2. In the Beginning the Neuron
   3. Structure of the Human Brain
II. Perception and Action
   4. Vision
   5. Audition
   6. Touch and Other Senses
   7. Movement
III. Forms of Awareness
   8. Sleep and Dreaming
   9. Attention
   10. Emotion and the Autonomic Nervous System
   11. Motivation
IV. Higher Processes
   12. Memory
   13. Frontal Lobe Functions
   14. Language
   15. Hemispheric Specialization
V. Breakdown of Higher Processes
   16. Amnesia and Disorders of Recognition

17. Breakdown of Language
18. Biological Aspects of Mental Illness
19. Senility and Dementia
20. The Elusive Right Hemishpere and the Pathology of Art

Units I-III include topics most frequently subsumed under the heading of physiological psychology and units IV and V will present topics most frequently taught under the title of neuropsychology. The incorporation of both elements, as documented, represents a perspective of human psychobiology that is comprehensive.

Expected outcomes are listed below and expanded in Appendix 6 for each module.

The student is expected to:

a) Acquire a basic knowledge of structures and functions of major neurological processes which aid the psychobiologist in studying behavior and consciousness.

b) Understand major theories of sleep, perception, emotion, motivation, memory, learning and language.

c) Comprehend basic controversies in contemporary psychobiology.

d) Understand the psychological application of anatomical, neuro-electrical, neurochemical, and neuroradiological methods.

e) Become familiar with assigned books and selected articles from professional journals describing psychobiological research.

f) Identify selected bioelectrical indices of the central nervous system and the autonomic nervous system.

g) Be able to write reports in the APA style and format.

PRODUCT AND UTILIZATION

Introduction to psychobiology was developed by the project director in 1977. In the past five quarters, the course has been taught three times with a total enrollment of 125 students. According to a survey, 40 percent were majors in psychology or biology, 30 percent were majors in health-related professions, and 30 percent were taking the course as an elective. This instructional package will not require updating for approximately five years. Based on annual student enrollments in the health-related professions as well as psychology and biology (see Appendix 7), it is anticipated that this program will reach 1,000+ students in this time. In addition, because of the mediated self-paced format, the program will be available to students for enrichment through the college seminar series offered by the Crestwood Individual Study Center.

APPROACH

It is the intent of this project to convert what is now a traditional course in psychobiology to a more versatile and visual-mediated self-instructional format focusing on human psychobiology. This would enable the course to be more accessible to Crestwood College students as well as other colleges. To accomplish this task the information must be developed into scripts for production. Learning objectives have been established for each of the 20 units (see Appendix 6). The scripts will be developed by the project director and will include the most recent research findings available in the field of human psychology. As an additional feature, certain information will be presented in the form of short commentaries, perspectives, enigmas, and controversies of the field. These commentaries will serve as a source of stimulation and creative exploration for the students.

An instructional design based upon Dr. Jerrold Kemp's (Kemp, 1975)[1] instructional design model will be utilized in preparation of the modules. The design model outlines the following:

a) Purpose
b) Student Group Characteristics
c) Learning Objectives
d) Subject Content
e) Teacher Activities
f) Student Activities
g) Resources
h) Support Services Needed
i) Evaluation Tools
j) Production Needs

This model will be constructed by the instructional development coordinator and the project director. The production team will convert the scripts into self-paced instructional modules utilizing the instructional design model. Through this cooperative effort, the unit content will be enhanced by the media format and the evaluation instruments and test content will parallel the intended objectives. All discipline content will be reviewed by consultants for accuracy and appropriateness. These consultants will advise on script revisions prior to final conversion to media format and on the appropriateness of visual materials.

PRODUCTION

The following production steps will be taken for each unit module:

1. Complete instructional design.

---

[1] Jerrold Kemp, Planning and Production of Audio Visual Material, 3rd ed., (New York: Crowell, 1975).

2. Convert lecture notes to script form.
3. Consultant evaluate scripts.
4. Edit scripts with input of instructional development team.
5. Match visuals and scripts onto storyboard cards.
6. Receive input on possible changes to storyboarded visuals.
7. Begin writing instructors' handbook and students' workbook.
8. Research available slides.
9. Send photographer out to location for original photography.
10. Have consent forms signed by all subjects of photographs.
11. Have title slides made by graphic artist.
12. Have charts and illustrations drawn up by illustrator.
13. Have film developed.
14. Collate slides into proper order.
15. Audiotape script narration.
16. Have original music developed.
17. Mix music, sound effects and narration on master audiocassette.
18. Sound synchronize slide tape show with inaudible signals for advancing.
19. Review slide tape with production team for any needed production refinement.
20. Complete packaging of materials and handbooks.
21. Consultant evaluate completed modules.
22. Form field testing groups, acquire students, implement three class groups and collect content evaluation data.
23. Review data for conclusive information.
24. Have instructors, students, and production specialists who were not involved in production evaluate aesthetics and format of materials.

EVALUATION

A two-phase evaluation will be conducted to determine the effectiveness of the completed materials. An evaluation instrument will be developed to measure the educational effectiveness and aesthetic qualities of the final product. This instrument will be developed from the following sources:

Gropper, George L., Tita Glasgow, and Jean Klingensmith. Criteria for the Selection and Use of Visuals in Instruction. Englewood Cliffs, N.J.: Educational Technology Publications, 1971.
Rahmlow, Harold F. "Using Student Performance Data for Improving Individualized Instructional Units," AV Communication Review, Vol. 19, Summer, 1975, pp. 169-183.
Wilson, Thomas C. "Behavioral Descriptors as a Means for More Effective Media Selection and Utilization," Educational Technology, Vol. 12, June, 1972, pp. 28-29.
Film and Video Tape Evaluation Form, Office of Middlesex County Superintendent of Schools, Brunswick Grove, N.J.: 1978.

Module-by-module evaluations will be made by students so that concept clarity can be increased. Overall content will be evaluated by consultants prior to conversion to final format.

The second phase of the evaluation will be conducted when the 20 modules have been completed. A pilot study will be conducted during the final quarter of the project to compare traditional instruction without SPI-M (control group), to traditional instruction with SPI-M supplement (experimental group 1), and SPI-M alone (experimental group 2). Pretests and posttests will be administered to all groups with data analyzed using analysis of variance.

BUDGET

	NSF	CRESTWOOD	TOTAL
Project Director			
Dr. Hank Kolakowski	7,500		7,500
$1,500/qtr. x 5 qtrs. = 1 class/qtr.			
Faculty and Other Associates			
Dolores Meyerhoff - Instructional Development		2,464	2,464
$6.16/hr. x 400 hrs.			
Paul Boren - Script Development/Editorial		711	711
$7.11/hr. x 100 hrs.			
John Emery - Production Assistant		2,276	2,276
$5.59/hr. x 400 hrs.			
Other Personnel			
Research Assistant	2,975		2,975
$5.72/hr. x 520 hrs.			
Illustrator	1,913	1,912	3,825
$7.65/hr. x 500 hrs.			
Photographer	3,150	600	3,750
3,000 slides @ $1.25/slide			
Narrator	1,600		1,600
40 hrs. @ $40/hr.			
Sound	1,000		1,000
Studio Time 40 hrs. @ $25/hr.			
Fringe Benefits	479	2,357	2,836
Materials and Supplies			
Slides - 20 programs of 200 slides	1,000		1,000
@ .25/slide			
4 copies of 20 programs - 2 copies slide/	1,350		1,350
tape; 2 copies video tape			
Tape - 3 cases ¼" tape and reels	250		250
Audiocassettes	100		100
Paper Copy	300		300
Graphic Supplies	500		500
Consultant	1,000		1,000
$25/hr. x 40 hrs.			
Total Direct Costs	23,117	10,320	33,437
Indirect Costs	1,849	3,698	5,547
TOTAL COST	24,966	14,018	38,984

Local Seismic Activity Learning Project

Lathan Community College District
Malec, Alaska 99552

      * Appendices   (not included)

      1. Exhibit A

      2. Exhibit B

      3. Exhibit C

      4. Exhibit D

      5. Curricula Vitae

Local Seismic Activity Learning Project

PROJECT SUMMARY

An examination of the existing geology program revealed that one weakness was the lack of direct laboratory experiences in some areas. For example, actual problem solving during units or movements of the earth's crust was not possible because actual local data of this movement was not available for the students. Although the college is in an area where faults and associated earthquakes are common, no working seismographs are available for use. With such local seismic data, existing courses will be modified to accommodate the greater emphasis on these reality-based lab problems.

The purchase and installation of a seismograph would also be a valuable addition to the instructional program of other departments within the science division, such as physics, astronomy, and the marine sciences. Funds are requested to purchase one short-period vertical seismometer, its accompanying seismograph, and a small amount of supporting instructional material. The seismograph will be installed in an area accessible to science students and their instructors, and will also be available for public viewing. With an on-campus seismograph it will be possible to implement the following project objectives: to modify course design in the 12 existing courses that will use local seismological data; to design and implement student learning exercises that involve using local seismological data and the seismograph; to develop and maintain a data base on local seismic activity which may be used in classroom instruction. Once these objectives are achieved, it is anticipated that student understanding of geological phenomena will be improved, student interest in the geology program will be increased, and the college will begin to become a geological information resource center for the community.

Introduction

The College

Located in southern Alaska, Lathan College serves the central regions of Corrine County, a district that covers 370 square miles and includes some of the newest communities in the United States. The population of Corrine County has expanded faster than any other area of Alaska and is still growing; 80-85 percent of this growth falls into Lathan's district, and college development has kept pace with that of the community.

In 1968 enrollment in the first class was 1,500. By the end of its first decade the college's still-growing enrollment will be 20,000, making it unique among post secondary institutions in the United States. This growth is projected to increase up to the year 2000 due to the continued development in 60 percent of Lathan's students who will transfer to four-year institutions. The student population is extremely diverse-- "traditional"

18- to 20- year-olds, vocational students, reentry women, military personnel from nearby bases, handicapped, and senior citizens (a retirement community of 15,000 sits at the college's doorstep). Currently the minority enrollment is 6.5 percent. All commute, and some from as far as 45 miles away. A satellite campus will open in spring 1979 to serve those who live in the northern-most sections of the district.

Need

A. The Natural Science Division

The natural science division is the second largest division on campus, with seven departments including geology/earth science, physics, astronomy, and marine sciences. The school's rapid growth has meant that divisional budgets have had to be stretched to provide staffing to keep up with the expanded student population. Attention has been focused on basic program content, and there has been little time or money to make long-rang plans, to upgrade curriculum, or to complete equipment purchases. In fall 1978, the division faculty decided to develop long-range plans based on a departmental needs assessment. The first department to complete this assessment was geology/earth science.

B. The Geology/Earth Sciences Department's Present Situation

Lathan's geology/earth science department has two full-time and several part-time instructors with a yearly enrollment of over 500 students. In addition to the six courses of the basic program, there are also two field courses and four general interest courses.

The geology/earth science department has already established excellent fossil, rock, and mineral collections including one representing all the geological provinces of Alaska and a local geological and paleontological collection. Students work with hand samples of rocks and minerals and examine simple geological models such as faults, folds, and stream tables. Geological displays outside the classroom that are also used for instruction include a geological calendar to scale (1 inch = 2.5 million years). An excellent slide collection, a spectrometer, and a lapidary laboratory all support student learning. A final important note is that the college property contains a fossil site, and plans are being formulated to protect it while using it for student learning.

When the teaching staff completed their departmental needs analysis, departmental goal setting became possible. As a result, four goals were established.

1. To upgrade the quality of geological education through actual,

124

as opposed to theoretical, problem solving.

2. To improve student understanding of geological phenomena.

3. To increase student interest in the program by addressing geological issues that are close at hand.

4. To become a geological information resource for the community.

The examination of the existing program revealed that one of the weaknesses of current instruction was its lack of direct laboratory experiences in some areas of the curriculum. For example, actual problem solving during units that discussed movements of the earth's crust was not possible because actual local data of this movement was not available for the students.

Southern Alaska is located in a section of the earthquake country that is of particular concern and of interest to all our community members and students. Our physical location offers us the opportunity to encourage advanced study and training in seismology and its relationship to plate tectonics, earth structure, and movements. Students and community alike need accurate, up-to-date information about earthquakes, particularly since there has been so much distorted, and often contradictory, information in the media and popular press.

Given these geological characteristics of Alaska and in light of the department's goals, the staff decided that a working seismograph would be a tool to obtain needed local seismic data and to help towards achieving the department's goals. It was also noted that a seismograph would be a valuable addition to the instruction program of other departments within the science division such as physics, astronomy, and the marine sciences. Therefore, obtaining a seismograph became a number one departmental priority.

Throughout Alaska's higher education institutions, seismographs are used to facilitate student learning in geology and related disciplines. Seismographs may also be found in community colleges and in museums and parks. However, there are no working seismographs convenient to Lathan College. In fact, the closest university does not even have a geology department.

Presently Lathan's geology labs are teaching basic seismic studies using either historical or hypothetical earthquake data. This data lacks the immediacy which arouses student interest, i.e., the earthquake tremor that students may have felt yesterday is more interesting than even the San Francisco quakes. Futhermore by seeing the graphic representation of yesterday's tremor and discussing it in class, students begin to want additional information and to ask thoughtful, comparative questions. It is this type of questioning, stimulated by the data from a local seismograph, that represents the beginning of basic earthquake knowledge.

The purpose of this proposal is to request funds to purchase one short-period vertical seismometer, its accompanying seismograph, and a small amount of supporting instructional material. The seismograph will be installed in an area accessible for use by science students and their instructors (see exhibit B), and will also be available for public viewing. The instructional materials will be used simultaneously in the classroom with additional material housed in the library for student review.

Project Description

Project goals will be accomplished through the implementation of the following objectives:

1. To modify course design in the 12 existing courses that will use local seismological data.

2. To design and implement student learning exercises that involve using local seismological data and seismograph.

3. To develop and maintain a data base on local seismic activity which may be used in classroom instruction.

Exhibit C contains current catalog descriptions of the 12 courses that are part of this project. The basis for all course changes will be to implement the goal of actual, as opposed to theoretical, problem solving and of greater student classroom participation. These planned curricula changes are also outlined in Exhibit C. Another project objective is to develop student learning exercises which will use the data provided by the seismograph and also train students in the operation of the seismograph. Both of the activities described above will be enhanced through the establishment and maintenance of a local seismic activity data base.

In addition to being a valuable learning tool, the seismograph can be an equally valuable means of enlightening and educating the community. It will be placed on public exhibition along with its accompanying explanatory displays. Humans are curious animals and few things attract their natural curiosities more than a seismograph. From merely watching the seismograph, the viewer moves to jumping up and down on the floor, trying to make it move, and then searches around for an explanation of what is happening.

Whether a seismograph is the spark that ignites an education in science, or whether it is part of an ongoing education from kindergarten to graduate school, it is one of the best education tools available.

Equipment

A.   Equipment Request

   Russell Williams, project director, conducted extensive research before
selecting the apparatus that would best suit the needs of Lathan College.
Geologists at the United States Geological Service and at several community
colleges within the state were contacted for their input. Using the above
criteria, the selection was narrowed to two vendors. Kinemetric equipment
was selected as being the best for the college, not only because the total
cost would be approximately $1,000 less than the other vendor's but also
because Kinemetric is nearer and would be easier to deal with, should problems
arise.

   The seismometer will be placed on bedrock, away from disturbances as much
as possible. A cable will connect this sensing device to the seismograph
(recording device) on the third floor in the foyer of the science/math
building. (It should be pointed out here that the third floor is also a
ground floor as this building is sunk into the side of a hill.) The seismograph will be kept running and available for everyone to see. In back
of the seismograph will be displays and maps showing how the machine works,
what it does, plots of recent earthquakes, recent seismograms of local and
distant earthquakes, and world maps and displays relating the seismograph
activity to plate tectonics (continental drift). One display will also
show how the composition of the earth's interior is studied through the use
of the seismograph (see Exhibit D).

B.   Equipment on Hand

   Presently the college has no seismographic equipment. However, two of
the maps to be used in the display are already on hand.

C.   Equipment Maintenance

   The natural science department has two full-time lab techinicians and
several part-time and temporary personnel. Wayne Wilkins is responsible
for the geological and physics equipment. After training by the project
director, he will be responsible for the instrument's maintenance, cleaning
and paper changes.

Evaluation

New course content areas developed using the newly available local seismic
data will go through a period of field testing before they are permanently
incorporated into the curriculum. Student learning exercises will be
similarly tested and modified according to student and instructor feedback.
The teaching faculty who are project participants will share their experiences in "localizing" the science curriculum in a division meeting.

Finally, the project director hopes that the installation of the seismograph will be the beginning step towards the establishment of a small science, math, and engineering museum.

Personnel

A. Faculty Expertise

Besides a master's degree in physical science, Russell Williams has had extensive experience with seismographs beginning in 1960. After completion of a seismology course at Juneau University, he went on to use and to train others to use seismographs in locations throughout the state.

He has published in the field and has had extensive teaching experience in geology, earth science, and marine science. He has also done consultant work for geologic engineering firms. His complete vita is in the appendix.

During the past year, the director has conducted a monthly series of community lectures entitled "Environment and Earth," based on various geological topics of interest to the public. He has also maintained a regular schedule of visits to elementary schools where he gives brief geology talks in the classroom.

Other instructors who will be using the seismograph are listed below and their complete vitae may be found in the appendix.

Kevin Ferguson, M. A. - Marine Science

Benjamin Bradley, M. A. - Physics

Kenneth Sollars, Ph. D. - Astronomy, Physics

Debra Pole, M. A. - Astronomy, Physics

Winifred Myrick, Ph. D. - Geology, Marine Sciences

Jacqui Easterland, M. A. - Marine Sciences

B. Information on Current or Proposed Projects

Three persons participating in this project are connected with other projects. Lathan has a pending physics grant whose project director is Kenneth Sollars and project participants are Debra Pole and Benjamin Bradley. If this project is funded, each participant will be grant funded for two person months in FY 1980 and Kenneth Sollars will be funded for an additional two person months in FY 1981. Participation in this grant does not represent a conflict of interest or double funding.

128

BUDGET

	Model	*Price	Subtotal
Scientific Equipment			
1. Kinemetric Seismograph (includes AC Time Mark)	VR-1	$2,231	
2. Kinemetric Seismometer (1 sec)	SS-1	682	
3. Kinemetric Filter (2 hz, 12 dg)	AF-1	184	
4. Radio Shack Time Cube	-	45	
5. Kinemetric Pen	-	26	
6. Cable (Belden 4 conductor)	9964, 8728	84	
			$3,252
Teaching Aids			
1. Maps for display cases	-	200	
2. Supplementary teaching materials	-	200	
			$ 400

Reference Materials

None

Construction of Equipment

1. Materials

    a. Materials to construct seismograph cabinet   300

    b. Materials to construct map display materials   175

                                                           $ 475

2. Labor

    a. Seismograph cabinet
        37 hours @ $9.50 per hour   350

    b. Map display
        16 hours @ $9.50 per hour   150

    c. Seismographic system installa-
        tion 37 hours @ 9.50 per hour   350

                                       $ 850

Hand and Machine Tools	None	
Computing Equipment	None	
Safety Equipment	None	

Expendable Items

1. Seismograph paper
    5 lots of 500   -   200

2. Seismograph ink   -   30   230

Freight Costs   75   75

Sales Tax for equipment costs
    4307 x .06   258

                        TOTAL EQUIPMENT COSTS $5,500

Amount provided by Lathan College District   - 2,700
                ($5,500 @ 50%)

                    Remainder from NSF $2,700

*   Prices quoted include an anticipated 5 % increase

TISSUE CULTURE DEVELOPMENT PROGRAM

Proposal to Conduct a Project Under
The Community College Endowment for Curriculum Development

Tissue Culture Development Program
Lisser Community College

TABLE OF CONTENTS

Lisser Community College

Tissue Culture Curriculum Development

Abstract

The intent of this project is to develop a curriculum in tissue culture practices (clonal propagation of plants). This will be accomplished through the development of a class in tissue culture techniques, the preparation of a training manual, and the establishment of a tissue culture laboratory in existing campus facilities. The project will provide for the training and skill upgrading of vocational students and professional nursery personnel and will create a needed source of trained technicians for the ornamental horticulture industry.

The outlined project will span a one-year period during which time the following objectives are to be accomplished: (1) initial consultation with an advisory committee consisting of tissue culture specialists and professional nursery personnel; (2) development of a course curriculum; (3) establishment of a tissue culture training facility; (4) preparation of a training manual; (5) supervision of course work and manual. It is expected that the benefits of this project will be ongoing, with the development curriculum becoming a permanent and regular part of our course offerings.

Project evaluation will be accomplished by the use of questionnaires addressed to industry representatives and students, by the tabulation of student enrollment and course completion, and by follow-up on the career progress of students through contact with employers and graduates. Project evaluation will continue beyond the tenure of this proposal.

TISSUE CULTURE PROGRAM DEVELOPMENT

Introduction

In the wholesale nursery profession tissue culture (the clonal propagation of plants) is the newest and most rapidly developing method of plant
production. Its application to the production of such previously hard-to-
propagate plants as orchids, ferns, bromeliads, and succulents has generated
considerable interest and profit in the industry. Nevertheless, the
movement of the nursery trade into this new area has been held back by a
shortage of qualified technicians. Presently no college, university, or
vocational institution in the Brathwaite County area is providing for the
training of tissue culture technicians, even though the leading agricultural
field in the county is the ornamental horticulture industry. With our ideal
climate for growing plants and the continued development of housing in the
county, it is expected that nursery work in ornamentals will expand and
that the need for trained personnel will increase.

The agricultural program at Lisser Community College began very modestly
in the spring semester of 1975 with the offering of two classes in general
horticulture. At that time a 1,000 square foot greenhouse served as our
sole laboratory. Although a few classes were added during the following
year, expansion did not begin in earnest until fall 1976. At that time the
curriculum was enlarged to include certificate programs in landscape design,
agricultural business, turfgrass practices, and ornamental horticulture.
Enrollment since 1976 has increased from 300 students per semester to
approximately 530. Average class size for 19 classes conducted in fall 1978
was 29.1. Presently the programs in ornamental horticulture and landscape
design are being emphasized. Facilities now include an additional greenhouse
of 6,400 square feet, a saranhouse of 5,500 square feet, two display gardens,
a student garden, soil bins, and one acre of growing grounds. Another 6
acres has been designated on campus for future use by the agriculture
department.

The proposed program will add a new dimension to our program and it was
the request of our agricultural advisory committee that this project be
undertaken.

Goals

This proposal provides for the expansion of the Lisser Community horticulture course offerings into the field of tissue culture (also called micro-
propagation of plants). The outlined program will (1) enable the development
of a curriculum adequate for the training of qualified tissue culture
technicians, (2) support the preparation of a training manual, and (3)
provide for the equipping and supplying of an operating tissue culture
facility on campus. No new construction, remodeling, or purchase of con-

struction materials is requested, but if such is needed for the ultimate completion of the described project, it will be provided from the annual operating budget of the agriculture department and not from this request. Laboratory space and shelving are available on the campus.

The project proposed will make it possible for vocational students and professional nursery personnel to acquire skills or skill upgrading in the use of this rapidly developing production method.

Specific Problem

In the local geographic area no training program currently takes the theories and techniques of tissue culture and applies them to a vocational technician training program. Training is available on a limited scale at a four-year level, but students enrolled in such programs are preprofessional graduate students who acquire the skills for research purposes. The commencement of tissue culture technician training is ideal for the community college agriculture curriculum and will become increasingly in demand.

Population to be Served

Enrollment in the proposed curriculum will include not only students preparing for entry into the nursery trade, but also a large number of nursery professionals interested in skill upgrading and skill acquisition. Roughly half of our current enrollment consists of working adults, many of whom wish to enter the field of ornamental horticulture for the first time. Military veterans comprise about 10 percent of our total enrollment.

It is expected that the proposed program will result in (1) the increased placement of students from Lisser Community College into the nursery profession as a result of this specialized and scarce training; (2) the in-service training of local nursery personnel; and (3) the development of a closer working relationship between the college agriculture program and the horticulture industry in the county.

Project Directorship

The directorship of the project will be shared by instructors George Brown and Martha Tate, Ph.D., full-time faculty members in the agriculture (ornamental horticulture) program at Lisser Community College. Consultation privileges, as needed, with the agricultural advisory committee (consisting largely of wholesale nursery personnel) and Herbert Cooper, Ph.D., and Glen Lomax, Ph.D. (tissue culture specialists) have been secured.

The Proposed Objectives of This Project

1. To develop a course curriculum for tissue culture technician-trainees.

2. To produce a laboratory manual to use in the tissue culture courses.

3. To teach students in tissue culture principles and skills and award a certificate of completion to students who complete and pass the course.

4. To equip and supply a tissue culture laboratory for tissue culture training.

5. To supply the needs of the nursery industry with qualified tissue culture technicians.

The Proposed Activities to Accomplish Objectives

1. At the beginning of the summer an agriculture advisory meeting will be held. Members of the agriculture advisory committee, nursery professionals, employed tissue culture technicians, and university professors specializing in plant physiology and micro-propagation will be invited. During the meeting the director team will initially identify the objectives of the tissue culture facility and ask those present to set up guidelines to use to evaluate the facility and students taking the course.

2. During the summer the director team will develop a course curriculum for training tissue culture technicians and order all necessary equipment and supplies to properly and adequately train students for the needs of the tissue culture industry.

3. During the fall semester the director team will develop a course manual for students. The manual will spell out objectives of the course, lecture material, and laboratory exercises covered throughout the course. Each exercise will feature a format containing a purpose, materials list, procedure, and a result and question section.

4. In January the in-service period (Lisser Community College is a pilot school on the 160-day calendar project) will be used to finish the manual and perform final revisions to assure that the manual will be available to the students at the beginning of the spring semester.

5. At the beginning of the spring semester the manual will be given to the students and used as a text-laboratory guide. Evaluation forms will be filled out by the students at the end of the course and turned in with their manuals.

6. During the last week of the spring semester the summary evaluation and manuals will be compiled by the director team and reviewed.

7. At the end of the spring semester an agriculture advisory meeting will be held. Participants of the first meeting will be invited, and the students' and director team's summary evaluations will be reviewed and discussed.

Expected Impact and Transferability

1. Since many wholesale nurseries are turning to tissue culture facilities for plant material or building their own laboratory, students completing the course will increase their chances of employment. It is expected that students from other disciplines (biology, botany, cellular biology, genetics, etc.) will enrich their knowledge on the principles of cellular reproduction, genetics, and plant physiology.

2. After setting up the tissue culture facility, courses in tissue culture will be offered every semester. The equipment and supplies for the facility, after the first year of operation, will be supported by the ornamental horticulture department at Lisser Community College.

3. This project will develop a model for training students in tissue culture practices. Since nurseries are expanding into the tissue culture area for plant material, it is expected that other community colleges and many wholesale nurseries will be interested in this project.

Evaluation Plan

1. Usage of the facility will be measured by the total enrollment of the students in the courses.

2. Students will be tested on their knowledge of the subject and their working skills in the laboratory. The lecture tests will consist of multiple-choice, true-false, fill-in, and essay questions, and the laboratory tests will consist of an oral and demonstration examination.

3. Questionnaires will be sent to nurseries that hire students as tissue culture technicians, asking them to evaluate the students' performance.

4. End-of-term evaluation forms will be filled out by the students and turned in with their manuals.

5. At the agriculture advisory meetings the director team will pass out to members present copies of the evaluation forms filled out by students, nursery professionals, and the director team. A review and discussion will follow. Any changes in the curriculum will be agreed upon by the members present.

Dissemination Plan

A manual, curriculum outline, and copies of all summary evaluations will be sent to the chancellor's office upon completion of the project. In addition, course fliers describing the program will be sent to nurseries and community colleges in the Brathwaite area.

BUDGET SUMMARY

	Local Funds	Endowment for Curriculum Development	Total
Professional Salaries	$2,560	$4,840	$7,400
Clerical Salaries	175	1,264	1,439
Employee Benefits	682		682
Books, Supplies, and Equipment Replacement		9,122	9,122
Other Direct Operating Expenses	300		300
Total Expenditures	$3,717	$15,226	$18,943

Arts
Humanities

JUNIOR COLLEGE CHORALE FOREIGN TOUR

CHORALE CHINA TOUR

A   Proposal to the

Dynasty Foundation

from

Goldston Junior College

Goldston, North Carolina

Introduction

Goldston Junior College is one of the twenty public community colleges in North Carolina. Both the college and the chorale began operating in 1960. The chorale consists of some sixty singers. During a given year, the chorale and its component organizations will give some fifty to sixty concerts at schools, clubs, churches, and conventions. In addition to these local concerts, the chorale travels abroad every other year. When the chorale is not traveling abroad, the group is touring through the United States.

Within the chorale there are three other organizations: The Barbershop Quartet, Madrigal Singers, and Jazz-Rock Vocal Ensemble. The Barbershop Quartet is a small male ensemble performing contemporary American music and has been widely received in the U.S. and Europe. The Madrigal Singers consist of twelve singers who sing chamber music from all major periods of music. The Jazz-Rock Vocal Ensemble consists of eight singers. Accompanying the chorale is a twenty-member instrumental jazz ensemble. All selections are staged and choreographed.

Among the performing credits of the chorale are the following:

1972   In this year the chorale first extended its scope of operation to the entire nation by embarking on a ten-state tour. Among other locations concerts were performed in the National Cathedral and the Capitol in Washington, D.C., and the Pan American Building in New York City.

1973   In the chorale's first international tour concerts were given during an eighteen-day visit to Europe. The chorale was awarded first place in an International Music Festival. This award followed a three-day competition with bands, orchestras, and choruses. The tour included concerts in London's St. James Cathedral, the Louvre and the American Cultural Center in Paris, the Chartre Cathedral near Paris, the Kaiser Wilhelm Lutheran Church in Berlin, and the Free University in West Berlin.

1975   The chorale's second overseas tour included Vienna, Austria, and the Soviet Union. The Vienna concerts were performed at the University of Vienna and at the St. Stephen's Cathedral. In Moscow a concert was given at the House of Friendship for Foreign Peoples; in Leningrad, at the Rimsky-Korsakov Conservatory.

1977   The chorale toured Italy, Greece, and Israel. The schedule included performances in the Greek Union Hall in Athens, Greece; the Kibbuts Auditorium, Gesher Haziv, Galilee, and Zionist Youth Auditorium in Jerusalem, Israel; and at

Theatre Societo San Paolo in Rome, Palizzio Vecchio Salon in Florence, and in the Church of San Moise in Venice, Italy.

Whether the annual tour is in the United States or overseas, the funding required is provided by donations solicited from community organizations (which have covered approximately one-half of the expenses) and by the chorale members themselves.

Proposed Tour

It is proposed that in the spring of 1980 the Goldston Junior College Chorale, accompanied by the instrumental jazz ensemble, tour China for fifteen days. The music performed in numerous concerts would be American contemporary including choral music with standard literature for full chorus. The performance schedule would be determined after consultation with appropriate Chinese officials.

Benefit to Chinese-American Relations

The Chorale has followed a practice of learning songs native to the countries visited. These songs are then performed in the various concerts given in the United States. Thousands of Americans have been exposed to foreign cultures through the native songs performed by the chorale. In order to understand the modern vocal and instrumental music of the Chinese more fully, chorale members would desire to attend workshops, lectures, and concerts dealing with the modern cultural aspects of Chinese music, dance, and song. Moreover, the college is the recipient of a U.S. Office of Education grant which is funding the residency of a Chinese curriculum consultant at the college for the 1979-80 academic year. This consultant would serve as a resource person to the chorale members before and after the concert tour. The consultant would insure that the native songs of China and the underlying culture are presented correctly by chorale members. All of the aforementioned activities would allow the students to present in a professional manner the modern cultural aspects of the Chinese choral and instrumental music, song, and dance.

The Chinese audience in attendance at each concert would of course be exposed to the spectrum of American music performed by the chorale, its component organizations, and the instrumental jazz ensemble.

Funds Requested

Air fare: Roundtrip - for sixty (60) students and two directors at $1,436 each = $89,032.

Food and lodging: $35 per day for 15 days for sixty (60) students and two directors = $32,550.

Travel within China: $15,000 for land travel by bus or train.

Total requested: $136,582.

GENERAL SUPPORT: ART GALLERY

PROPOSAL FOR UNRESTRICTED SUPPORT OF

THE PLAINFIELD SCHOOL OF ART

Philadelphia, PA

PROPOSAL FOR UNRESTRICTED SUPPORT OF

THE PLAINFIELD SCHOOL OF ART

INTRODUCTION

The Plainfield School of Art is one of the oldest art schools in the country as well as the only professional studio art school in the city of Pittsburgh. Since its founding in 1890, the Plainfield School has grown from one volunteer instructor and a handful of students to 65 faculty members and a student body of 1,000. As an integral part of the Plainfield Gallery, the school is known for its professionalism, its innovative approaches to art education, and its commitment to training young artists. At the same time, the school has tried to keep tuition at an accessible rate for talented students of all income levels.

Established and nurtured by private enterprise, the Plainfield School and Gallery guided the cultural life of Pittsburgh long before it became a city of museums. Except for direct financial aid to students, the school receives no federal funding, nor does it receive any support from city or county sources. Now demand is growing for professional education in the arts and the school must seek additional funds to assure that mounting costs will not require cutbacks that would affect the quality of the education offered.

ABOUT THE SCHOOL

The school offers two accredited programs for full-time study which lead to a diploma in fine arts, visual communications, or photography, or a bachelor of fine arts degree. The "Open Program" accommodates part-time nondegree students. Over the last nine years part-time students numbered 8,000; summer school students over 2,000; and 3,000 have enrolled in Saturday school which serves adults and youths aged 11-18. In the 1979 fall semester, the school enrolled 207 full-time students, 400 part-time students, and 110 Saturday school students. Over 80 percent of the school's alumni have established themselves as successful exhibiting artists, graphic designers, free-lance artists, and professional photographers.

Students are taught by a faculty of 65 practicing artists and designers of national reputation. Studios for ceramics, sculpture, water color, and design are located in the school as well as photography labs, printmaking facilities, and wood and machine workshops. In many ways the gallery serves as the school's largest classroom where students can evaluate their work against the artistic excellence represented in the Plainfield collection. For research and study, students use the curatorial library of the gallery and the school's library, which holds an extensive slide collection, several thousand volumes, and a wide selection of periodicals.

In addition the school offers many exciting opportunities for students to become involved in activities outside the classroom. The advantages of the art school's association with a nationally acclaimed gallery are many. This year the art students were invited to make ornaments for the State House Christmas tree. They also made costumes and decorations for the Plainfield's masquerade, a major Pennsylvania social event. Other students work as interns in the gallery or earn tuition money by assisting in the museum's offices or with special events. Another noteworthy feature of the school's curriculum is the visiting artists program in which esteemed artists, dealers, authors, and scholars are invited to speak and work with Plainfield students throughout the year.

THE NEED

At his death in 1888 William Plainfield established the art school with an endowment of $100,000 which to this day remains the only large fund restricted for the school. The "entrance fee" was either free or nominal before 1947, and the school has supported itself chiefly through tuition revenue since then. Even today tuition income is 85 percent of its revenue. However, the school now shares the pressures, common among other educational institutions, of escalating operating costs.

Tuition has increased 31 percent over the past decade as the school's expenses have doubled. Consideration has been given to raising tuition again to meet next year's projected deficits, but another tuition increase would deny enrollment to many deserving students from middle- and lower-income families who make up a large percentage of the school's enrollment. The school itself makes an effort to assist needy students by providing about $33,000 annually in scholarship aid.

Because it has been self-supporting, the school has a limited history of fund raising and has no organized alumni body. The school receives no federal, local, or county funds, nor can Pittsburgh depend on the corporate resources that finance arts institutions in other cities with major industries. Whereas once tuition and modest donations could cover the school's expenses, we are entering a new decade in which tuition must be augmented substantially to maintain the same financial stability. The need is urgent and clear-cut.

CONCLUSION

A grant to the Plainfield School of Art would support both the Pittsburgh community and the nation. While encouraging the development of young artists, the gift would promote the cultural growth and enrichment of the state's capital and the accessibility of art education to lower- and middle-come students. The Plainfield has received a challenge grant from the Rinick Foundation, and as a result, your gift would double the income to the school.

Your contribution would be acknowleged in our literature as well as inside the gallery and the school. The director of the gallery and the dean of the Plainfield School would welcome the chance to show you around the school and to respond to your further questions and observations.

EDUCATIONAL PROGRAM: ART GALLERY

A request for

Financial Support for the

Richardson Art Gallery

from the

Zimmers Foundation

The following proposal describes a new program developed by the education department of the Richardson Art Gallery for use in Philadelphia, Pa. area schools. Discover America at the Richardson is an interdisciplinary program for elementary and high school students which explores the relationship of American Art, history, and literature through audio-visual presentations in the classroom and activities led by a docent in the Richardson Gallery. The Richardson Art Gallery requests $15,000 from the Zimmers Foundation to support this program which will improve the quality of cultural education in the schools and enrich the community at large.

DISCOVERY UNITS

NEED

Our contacts with area teachers indicate that cultural enrichment programs are being cut back as a result of surging transportation costs and budget stringencies. Unfortunately, it seems that students attending schools in areas where such enrichment is most needed are the ones most often deprived of the chance to participate in such programs. Museum programs could supplement the shortcomings of cultural education in the schools, but museums have not responded to these needs for the most part. The museum program proposed here attempts to broaden the limiting classroom experience by providing select visual stimulation and the guidance of cultural specialists.

THE PROGRAMS

Discover America at the Richardson is designed to complement humanities classes in secondary and elementary schools. The paintings in the Richardson's collections provide visual counterparts to students' lessons in History, English, and American studies. The two units of this program--"Face to Face" and "Dialogue With Nature"--have been developed with the flexibility to fit into the curriculum of many area schools for the 1979-80 school year.

The units will be presented as two-part programs whenever possible, consisting of a classroom presentation and a gallery tour. For schools that participate in the gallery tour only, learning packets are sent to teachers that include ideas for independent classroom activities.

"Face to Face" uses the Richardson's extensive collection of colonial portraits to introduce elementary school students (grades 2 through 6) to the men and women who represent American history. A docent visits the classroom and helps the students explore questions such as, "What is a portrait? What do clothing, gestures, and props reveal about the sitter? What kind of person would have had his portrait painted in 1750...1860...1970?" A slide presentation is followed by role plays in which the children draw a portrait of a colonial figure. Aside from the obvious enrichment to the study of history, classroom activities encompass exercises in the basic skills of reading, writing, and spelling.

Students visiting the gallery will see firsthand the wide range of portraits in the Richardson's collections. For some of these children, it will be their first experience in a museum or gallery. The program attempts to provide both fun and education. In mime games, students trace the changing ways in which artists have portrayed their contemporaries throughout American history.

"Dialogue With Nature" is designed for high school students and focuses on the literature and thought of nineteenth century America as reflected in the Richardson's outstanding collection of nineteenth century landscape paintings. As in "Face to Face," a docent will use slides to make connections between the work of American writers such as Emerson, Melville, Hawthorne and Whitman, and Hudson River School paintings by Thomas Cole, Frederic Church and Albert Bierstadt. Role playing exercises will encourage students to think about nature as the writers, artists, and settlers of the nineteenth century would have.

At the gallery, students will see the impact of landscape paintings in the greater context of American art. Through close inspection, they can analyze methods that artists used to convey their visions of Romanticism and the exploration of the great West. In addition, the bibliography and suggested reading assignments which supplement "Dialogue With Nature" can be used by teachers to develop a major unit on nineteenth century American literature and cultural history.

BENEFITS TO STUDENTS

Discover America at the Richardson is an ambitious program which would for the first time, bring the resources of the Richardson to people who might otherwise never reap the museum's benefits. Teachers indicate that this type of outreach program is not available through any other major Philadelphia museum.

By exposing students to the visual counterparts of what they study in the classroom, the education department hopes to enrich the study of American culture and create an awareness of art as a conscious reflection of the values of that culture. Both programs not only heighten academic skills, but teach students the value of discussion and the process of formulating opinions and making judgements. Gallery and classroom activities also demonstrate to students that what they think and say is important, since many of the exercises focus on their observations and conclusions.

METHOD

The Richardson Education Department developed the Discover America at the Richardson unit during the 1978-79 school year. Elaine Lahaska, curator of education, contacted the heads of the Philadelphia departments of art, history, and English to determine the need for the proposed projects. The units were developed with the expressed support of the Philadelphia school system and its outlying suburbs.

Seth Alan, assistant professor of English at Temple University last year, served as a consultant in researching and writing the basic materials for the units. Mr. Alan worked closely with a curriculum specialist in the Bucks County Schools on this task.

Currently, the curator of education, her assistant, and secretary are working almost full-time to prepare the program for testing in the schools this year. The essay and activities are being refined and printed. Philadelphia teachers are learning about the new units through workshops where the programs are demonstrated and discussed. A selected group of Richardson docents are being trained to give classroom presentations and tours. Training includes readings of eighteenth and nineteenth century literature, lectures by consultants, and pilot presentations by the education staff.

EVALUATION

Two forms will be used to evaluate the program. The student evaluation will elicit suggestions and individual reactions to the program. Teachers will assess the success of the unit in three areas:

1) degree of appropriateness to existing curriculum

2) enrichement value to existing curriculum

3) learning opportunities presented to the class as a group and as individuals.

Revisions to units will be based on these evaluations.

After a test period of one year, evaluations and results will be tabulated by a committee composed of the project director, educational consultant, selected docents, and classroom teachers.

LONG-RANGE COMMUNITY BENEFITS

"Face to Face" and "Dialogue With Nature" can become important, permanent components of the education department's school programs. In terms of budget, the program is ideal. Initial outlays for purchasing drawing and audio-visual materials will be the major cost. Yearly costs thereafter will be minimal--only additional printing and mileage costs for docents driving to schools.

The program also is broad enough to benefit other segments of the population besides students. For example, by changing the focus and activities slightly, an excellant program on the history and art of America could be produced for senior citizens. This large segment of the public has difficulty traveling to the gallery, but appreciates good programming which can be brought to their facilities.

MODEL PROGRAM

As a model program, Discover America at the Richardson will meet the present and future needs of teachers and students, serve as a pilot project for museum endeavors nationally, and offer opportunities for expansion in a cost-efficient manner. This is a new direction for the Richardson and one which other museums may soon realize they must follow. Information on the program can be disseminated through museum education communiques.

REQUEST

With assistance from the Zimmers Foundation, all of these activities can be implemented. Fliers can be sent to teachers of English, history and art, and more workshops can be held to publicize the units to teachers. Additional docents can be trained to work in the classroom and give tours as the number of students that come to the Richardson increase. Slide projectors, slides, costumes, paper and crayons can be purchased for the classroom presentation, and 1,000 copies of each unit can be printed.

This program is not yet fully operative. A Zimmers Foundation grant can make it possible for the Richardson to get to the schools, to bring students to the museum, and to add exciting learning materials to the curriculum. To the community, a grant from the Zimmers Foundation would mean new opportunities for cultural enrichment and growth.